The Cultural World of Jesus

The Cultural World of Jesus

Sunday by Sunday

Cycle B

John J. Pilch

A Liturgical Press Book

 THE LITURGICAL PRESS
Collegeville, Minnesota

2	3	4	5	6	7	8

Library of Congress Cataloging-in-Publication Data

Pilch, John J.
    The cultural world of Jesus : Sunday by Sunday / John J. Pilch
        p. cm.
    Includes bibliographical references.
    Contents: [1] Cycle B
    ISBN 0-8146-2287-9 (cycle B)
    1. Bible N.T. Gospels–Liturgical lessons, English. 2. Bible.
N.T. Gospels–Meditations. 3. Bible. N.T. Gospels–History
of Biblical events. 4. Middle East–Civilization. I. Title.
BX2170.C55P49   1994
264'.34–dc20   94-44772
                                                        CIP

For Benjamin R. Baran

אִישׁ שְׁלוֹמִי

(Psalm 41:10)

Scholar and Teacher Extraordinaire

Contents

Introduction

The idea for these reflections from a Mediterranean cultural perspective on the Gospel read at Sunday liturgies originated in a monthly column I wrote for *Modern Liturgy* between 1989 and 1991. When my tenure as columnist ended, I persuaded Initiatives Etc., of Columbus, Ohio, to publish a brief weekly reflection on a subscription basis.

This one-page bulletin-insert quickly became very popular with adult enrichment and RCIA groups. I have been delighted when visiting parishes to conduct Bible study seminars to see parishioners diligently reading the insert and checking the missalette before Mass.

It has been even more satisfying to hear the preacher say: "My topic this morning is x. Other interesting ideas about today's Gospel can be found in the bulletin insert. I encourage you to read and reflect on that page with your Bible at home. For this morning, however, let us reflect on my topic, x." Often the preacher further develops a topic from the insert and makes significantly appropriate applications to the local community.

This collection of reflections is revised and slightly larger than the subscription series. The architects of the Lectionary have provided readings for fifty-six Sundays in each year's Cycle. No liturgical year lasts fifty-six weeks. Lent, Easter, and other feasts cause various Sundays to be omitted each year. This collection treats only the Gospels assigned for the fifty-six Sundays as found in the Lectionary. It does not include the Gospels for feasts that sometimes fall on a Sunday.

The Interpretation of the Bible in the Church, published in 1993 by the Pontifical Biblical Commission, highlighted some distinctive insights that Mediterranean cultural anthropology can shed on interpreting the Bible. The concepts enumerated in these paragraphs reflect the publications of The Context Group, an association of biblical scholars of which I am a charter member. For nearly two decades this group has dedicated itself to studying the Mediterranean backgrounds of the New Testament. The Biblical Commission's document represents concepts developed in research papers read by Context Group members at a scientific meeting in Spain in 1991. The list of recommended readings that concludes this volume reports these ground-breaking studies whose insights are liberally reflected in my reflections.

I have not listed the excellent Gospel commentaries and commentaries on the Lectionary that adopt other approaches and are readily available for anyone desiring a more comprehensive treatment of these texts. The focus here is almost exclusively on the Mediterranean cultural perspective.

Purists or sensates on the Myers-Briggs scale may object to the global adjective "Mediterranean." They will correctly insist on recognizing the differences of each country in this part of the world. Nevertheless, reputable specialists in Mediterranean culture convincingly demonstrate that this region (which they sometimes call "Circum-Mediterranean"– see George Foster, *Culture and Conquest* [Chicago: Quadrangle Books, 1960] 25) share many cultural elements unchanged over several millennia. The core values of honor and shame are two such basic elements. Details of honorable and shameful behavior do indeed differ from country to country. These reflections present the characteristics of the first-century eastern Mediterranean region.

Thus, I use the words "Mediterranean" or "Middle Eastern" precisely to describe the culture of the people who populate, and whose lives are reflected in, the Bible. The insights about the culture of this world are derived from contemporary anthropological investigations, particularly the research of Mediterranean anthropologists such as Lila Abu-Lughod, Camillia Fawzi El-Solh, Soraya Altorki, Elizabeth Warnock Fernea, David Gilmore, and members of The Context Group.

Anthropologists agree that the judicious use of contemporary data, linked to historical accounts, is basic and reliable anthropological methodology (see Foster, *Culture and Conquest,* 30). It is legitimate anthropological method to retroject contemporary insights over two and three thousand years because, until the advent of colonialism and the discovery of oil and its consequences, the culture of the region remained remarkably unchanged.

In sum, these reflections are an attempt to fulfill the exhortations of the Second Vatican Council, which urged interpreters of the Bible to pay due attention to "the characteristic styles of perceiving" that prevailed at the time of the sacred author (On Revelation, no. 12). Perception is governed by culture. The better an interpreter knows the culture in which the Bible originated, the more culturally plausible will be the interpretation.

It is exactly this understanding that stands behind the instruction for preachers that cautions: "When they narrate biblical events, let them not add imaginative details which are not consonant with the truth" (The 1964 Instruction on the Historical Truth of the Gospels, par. XIII). The phrase "consonant with the truth" is best rendered "culturally plausible."

Moreover, *The Interpretation of the Bible in the Church* urges preachers to focus on the central contribution of Lectionary texts in order to actualize and inculturate the text appropriately in the lives of the listeners. The approach of cultural anthropology that characterizes the reflections in this book is admirably suited to helping achieve this goal in the liturgy.

Preachers are fond of quoting the literal Greek translation from John's Gospel, that Jesus "became human and pitched his tent among us" (1:14). Specifically and in the concrete, Jesus was a first-century, Middle Eastern peasant, driven by the core cultural values of honor and shame, expert in the art of challenge and riposte, and master of all his culture's strategies. The challenge to Western believers is to understand and appreciate Jesus on his own terms. To this I hope my reflections make some modest contribution.

Feast of the Portiuncula   John J. Pilch
August 2, 1996   Georgetown University

First Sunday of Advent
Mark 13:33-37

According to Mark's Jesus, nobody knows about "that day or hour" in which the Son of Man will return, neither the angels in heaven, nor Jesus himself, but only the Father (v. 32). Yet Jesus assured his immediate audience that they would not "pass away until all these things have taken place" (v. 30). His thrice-repeated exhortation, "keep awake, stay alert," highlights the urgency of the situation.

To appreciate Jesus' exhortation, a modern Western reader needs to understand the Middle Eastern view of time and the relationships between master and servants.

TIME

Mediterranean cultures are oriented primarily to the present. Future events are very difficult to imagine and nearly impossible to grasp. Activities that do not have to take place at the present moment (e.g., cooking the next meal, getting dressed to start the day) are routinely put off. For the Spaniards there is *mañana,* and for the Italians, *domani.* The popular song lyrics say, "Let's forget about *domani.*" Even Jesus reminded his followers not to "worry about tomorrow, for tomorrow will have worries of its own. Today's trouble is enough for today" (Matt 6:34).

Yet the Middle Eastern concept of the present includes tomorrow. Jesus taught his believers to pray: "Give us tomorrow's bread today" (Matt 6:11; Luke 11:3).

So what is the point in today's gospel? In Mark 13, Jesus has announced an event that is imminent, along with its

1

accompanying signs. But none of these signs was yet visible to his listeners, and the normal cultural tendency would be to put such an exhortation and event out of mind. "Today's trouble is enough for today."

People with a strong cultural orientation to the present need to be nudged to think more about the future, even if only tomorrow, just as Americans whose cultural orientation is primarily toward the future need to be reminded to think about the present, today, this very moment.

MASTER AND SLAVES

It is important to translate the word here as "slave" and not "servant," because in the first-century world these people were indeed "slaves," that is property of the owner. At the same time, Americans must realize that "slavery" in the ancient Mediterranean world had nothing in common with New World slavery.

The relationship of dominance and dependency characteristic of slavery was regulated by varied and extensive laws and legal traditions in all the Mediterranean cultures that thrived in the New Testament period. The institution was so prevalent, it was easily adopted into faith traditions as well.

Ancient Israelites viewed themselves as "slaves of God" because the Lord had liberated them or their ancestors from bondage in Egypt (Lev 25:55). Freeborn persons in the New Testament period who became Christians viewed themselves as having become "slaves of Christ" (1 Cor 7:22) or "slaves of God" (1 Pet 2:16).

Further, because the Mediterranean cultures are group centered, the slave's worth derived from the group served. All the slaves mentioned in the New Testament are members of an extended household. This means they are considered to be members of the family. Accordingly, Christian slaves are cautioned against taking advantage of being "brothers" or "sisters" of Christian owners but are instead to "serve all the better" (1 Tim 6:2).

It is precisely the slave's status as member of an extended household that helps a modern believer to grasp the importance of Jesus' parable. These slaves are family. The master who goes on a long journey expects every member of the household, every family member, to do the work they are assigned (v. 34). They must not put it off for tomorrow.

The doorkeeper, too, is to keep watch for the master's return, lest he find the family fast asleep instead of eager to greet and welcome the returning head of household. Anyone who has returned home after a long absence at a late hour knows the difference between being greeted by a loved one and entering a house where all are asleep.

Mark's Jesus urges his listeners and subsequent generations of believers to be ever watchful for the return of a beloved family member. It is, after all, a fact of our faith: the beloved Master will indeed return and expect to be welcomed by family in fitting fashion. Are we ready?

Second Sunday of Advent
Mark 1:1-8

Unlike Matthew and Luke, Mark reports no genealogy for Jesus, yet he accomplishes the same thing they do: establishing Jesus' honorable status and authority.

SON OF GOD

The word commonly translated "gospel" in verse 1 ("the beginning of the *gospel* of Jesus the Messiah") is more fittingly translated "proclamation."

Ancient Mediterranean people were familiar with proclamations. They were generally made on behalf of or about rulers (e.g., announcing the birth of a new ruler, reporting a recent military victory by the ruler). Mediterranean people would immediately wonder: who is this Jesus, and by what right does he make proclamations?

If this person is simply Jesus of Nazareth in Galilee (Mark 1:9), he would have little claim to honor. Recall Nathanael's incredulous question: "Can anything honorable come out of Nazareth?" (John 1:46). A village artisan has no authority to make proclamations.

Mark has a ready answer: Jesus is Son of God. This statement announces Jesus' status, the basis of his acquired honor by reason of which he can speak and act on behalf of God.

The Second Vatican Council's Dogmatic Constitution on Divine Revelation (no. 12) urges all who interpret the Bible to "investigate what the sacred writer intended to express and actually expressed." Mark actually expressed the phrase "Son of God." What did he intend to express?

4

In Hebrew and other Semitic languages, the phrase "son of so-and-so" means "having the qualities of so-and-so." The phrase "son of man" means having the qualities of a man or person, hence in a word it means "human." The ancients understood thunder as the voice of God (see Ps 29:3-9), hence "sons of thunder" describes "those who echo the voice of God" (see Mark 3:17). A son of God is one who has "the quality or qualities of God," hence one who is divine or divine-like. This is more than sufficient justification for Jesus' behavior as a proclaimer.

MARK

And who is this person who presumes to narrate the story of this extraordinary Jesus? What do we know about him? The gospel does not identify its author, but tradition (since Papias) has suggested a certain "Mark," companion of Peter in Rome (1 Pet 5:13). The belief is that Peter or his recollections stand behind this gospel no matter who "Mark" really is.

From a cultural perspective, that would be beside the point. Whatever his identity, this author presents an honorable personal status as strong as Jesus' status. In the second verse, the evangelist demonstrates ability to quote Scripture creatively. While citing explicitly only Isaiah, he has also included Malachi, demonstrating not only familiarity with the sacred traditions but creative ability to reshape them. Such skill was immediately recognized, highly regarded, and admired.

JOHN THE BAPTIZER

The third honorable figure to appear in this prologue is dressed like Elijah (v. 6; see 1 Kgs 1:8), preaches reform, and announces the advent of the Messiah. Yet for all his boldness, the Baptizer displays the appropriate and expected cultural humility. He describes the coming one as "more powerful than me" and declares himself "not worthy to stoop down and untie the thong of his sandals" (v. 7). An honorable person never presumes to usurp the honor of another.

As a preacher, John is a smashing success. He addresses head on the day-to-day concerns of his predominantly peasant audience. The theme of John's preaching was "remission of debts" (translated "forgiveness of sins"). Jesus echoed this in the Lord's Prayer: "forgive us our debts as we forgive our debtors" (Matt 6:12; Luke 11:4).

Peasants from the Judean countryside were deeply in debt. In first-century Palestine, as much as 35 to 40 percent of total agricultural production was eaten up by a variety of taxes. Peasants unable to pay lost ownership of the land and became sharecroppers. As demands on them became even greater, many fled the land. Many became artisans. Thus, artisans and non-elites from Jerusalem were not much better off than the peasants.

That honorable preachers like John and Jesus would proclaim remission of debts is good news. Advent is an opportune time for all Christians to address the burning issues of life courageously.

Third Sunday of Advent
John 1:6-8, 19-28

PRIEST OR PROPHET?

Why should the religious authorities in Jerusalem show concern for a marginal figure attracting crowds to the wilderness and baptizing repentant sinners in the Jordan?

In cultures guided by honor, persons are expected to behave according to their inherited status. The Baptizer's status or acquired honor derived from the fact that his father, Zechariah, was a devout rural priest.

But the Baptizer is not behaving like a priest. Instead, he looks very much like a member of the numerous groups of alienated priests that emerged as early as the sixth century B.C.E. These groups found themselves increasingly separated from the aristocratic priests in Jerusalem. The historian Josephus indicates that the gulf between the latter and the large number of lower clergy was very great just before the outbreak of the Judaic rebellion against Rome in the mid-sixties C.E.

A major cause of alienation was the widely known and very evident luxury in which the Jerusalem priestly aristocracy lived in contrast to the conditions of the rural clergy. In 1976, a report on excavations in the Jewish Quarter of the Old City of Jerusalem described a Herodian house of two thousand square feet, and a larger one the excavators called "The Mansion." In the mansion they found a stone with the name "Bar Kathros," one of four priestly families described in the Talmud (*Pesah* 57a) as exploiting the people and beating them with rods. The contents of these homes together with their unusually large size illustrates the luxury of the Jerusalem aristocracy in the first century.

By his dress and diet, the Baptizer distances himself from this luxury and his rural priestly heritage and presents himself more like a prophet, a spokesperson who declares the will of God for the here and now. The Jerusalem priests wonder whether John is an "action prophet" (a spokesperson who also leads a popular movement hoping that God will intervene in liberating action) or an "oracular prophet" (one who only pronounces words of redemption or judgment).

After interrogating John, the delegation from the Jerusalem authorities conclude that he is only an oracular prophet. He explicitly says he is not the light but only the witness to the light. He denies that he is the Messiah, Elijah, or "the prophet" who was to return at the end of time. He is but the voice crying in the wilderness exhorting his listeners to prepare the way of the Lord. Because Jesus has not yet been baptized nor initiated his ministry, the delegation isn't interested in the "coming one" John announces.

REFORM AND BAPTISM

The second concern of the delegation is John's baptism. "If you are not one of these expected figures, then why do you baptize?"

Baptism was rather common in antiquity even outside of Judaism. The mystery cults of Isis, Mithras, and Eleusis contained baptismal rites. In the Old Testament, Naaman was cleansed of his skin problem by bathing in the Jordan (2 Kgs 5:14). The high priest was required to engage in a purification rite before and after the rites of atonement (Lev 16:4, 24), and Leviticus 15 prescribes it for menstruating women. The Qumran community, too, practiced a form of baptism. In each case, the meaning of the baptismal rite derives from the ritual context, or instruction, or tradition.

The Jerusalem delegation understands John's baptismal rite to be a symbolic action. They want to know what it means. Mark and Luke identify it as a "baptism of repentance for the forgiveness of sins," a rite symbolizing purification and cleansing, a return to God.

The evangelist John implies yet another dimension. The Baptist baptizes with water, but one who is to come after him will bring a more radical purification to those willing to repent (see Luke 3:16-17).

Americans can comprehend this more radical reform by drawing an analogy with contemporary efforts to reform the American health-care system. Current ideas echo many that were proposed by reformers but defeated over the past twenty years. Current conditions require more radical reforms. Ultimately, "one who is stronger" will succeed.

Fourth Sunday of Advent
Luke 1:26-38

VIRGINITY AND HONOR

In the ancient Mediterranean world, people believed that unless prevented by appropriate measures, a man and a woman who found themselves alone together would inevitably have sexual relations. This is why the culture prescribes that men (fathers, husbands, brothers) watch, guard, and protect the women in their care (Sir 26:10-12).

There are a variety of strategies for carrying out this concern. One is to ensure that a woman is always in the company of other women and children (girls and boys) younger than the age of puberty. Another is the structure of the houses where the inner room or courtyard secluded from the view of people (men) in the outside world is reserved as the proper place for unmarried women.

In Luke's account of the annunciation, a presumably masculine angel visits Mary who seems to be quite alone. Very likely, she is in the innermost quarters of her family's home, the proper place for an unmarried young woman. The angel is an intruder, and the scene would strike any Mediterranean person as suspicious, angel notwithstanding.

Moreover, Mary is betrothed (a more accurate word than the misleading "engaged") to Joseph. Betrothal was a family event rather than an event between two individuals. Marriage in the ancient Middle East was arranged by the parents with the intention of joining and strengthening two families. In Middle Eastern villages today, the marriage contract is negotiated by the mothers to make certain the families are of equal status and that neither family is taking advantage of the other. The patriarchs will ultimately ratify what has been negotiated.

Mary thus finds herself in an embarrassing and potentially shameful situation. Should anything happen to her in the family home, her father and brothers would be shamed for not taking proper care of her (see Sir 42:9-10). The family's shame would increase on the marriage evening if no tokens of virginity could be produced (see Deut 22:13-21).

It is interesting to examine paintings of this scene by Mediterranean artists. Mary invariably holds her hands up in a defensive gesture. The angel is separated from Mary by a prie-dieu, or a doorway, or a similar solid object. There must be some indication that honor is not being compromised.

The honorable angel first recognizes her honorable status: "Greetings, favored one! The Lord is with you!" Then this male intruder sets her at ease ("Do not be afraid") and proceeds to explain God's will for her.

Notice that despite all the honorable assurances from the messenger, Mary is still properly concerned about her honor status: "How can this be, since I am a virgin?" She is fully aware of the significance and consequences of the angel's message. In a flash, she recognizes the new challenges that will emerge in her betrothal and the crisis into which this pregnancy could throw both families (see Deut 22:13-21 and Num 5:11-31).

The angel reminds Mary, "Nothing is impossible with God." Mediterraneans recognize in the angel's explanation two indications that God is going to play the role of traditional husband for Mary. He will "empower" her ("the spirit will come upon you") and "protect" her ("overshadow you"), two duties of a Middle Eastern husband. The meaning is not lost on Mary, the Mediterranean maiden.

Her concluding remark is a typical Middle Eastern cultural response when one has lost an argument, or decides to conclude a discussion that is going nowhere. The sentiment "let it be done to me according to your word" is more commonly stated, "As you wish." At this stage of the story, there still remains much for Mary to face. She may be as perplexed after the angel departs as she was when he arrived.

Historians frequently point to figures in the ancient world whose origins sound just like Jesus'. For instance, Asclepius, the healing deity, had a human mother, Coronis (or Arsinoe), and a divine father, Apollo. From their twentieth-century, theologically enlightened perspective, modern Christians find the fact that Jesus had no human father not to be troubling.

Attempting to enter the first-century world and culture of Palestine to understand and appreciate this scene in Luke leads to a more sympathetic view of the unsettling experience it must have been for Mary. Even for saints, faith is not easy.

Holy Family
Luke 2:22-40

Defining the family is never easy. The challenge was no different in the ancient world than it is in modern cultures. Even more difficult is deciding what kind of family is good and decent, and what kind of family is not.

As today's gospel indicates, the family into which Jesus was born and raised is unquestionably devout and pious. They observe the Torah meticulously. In accord with Leviticus 12:3, Jesus' parents have him circumcised and name him on the eighth day after he is born. In accord with the larger context of Leviticus 12:1-8, the family accompanies Mary to the Temple in Jerusalem for her purification forty days after the birth of Jesus.

CIRCUMCISION AND NAMING

In the ancient Middle East, circumcision was practiced in many societies. Its origins are obscure. Originally, scholars thought it had originated in Egypt and moved thence east and north into the Semitic world. Contemporary opinion rooted in recent archaeological discoveries holds that the practice of circumcision began in the northwest Semitic world and moved south where the Egyptians adopted it.

The meaning of the procedure varied. For instance, in early Israelite history, males were circumcised at puberty (see Gen 17:25) or at the time of marriage (Gen 34). In this connection, the rite has a functional meaning: the man is now able to get married and to function as a married person.

It was not until Abraham was circumcised that Sarah was able to bear a child, the proper child whom God would bless.

Later in Israelite history (see Lev 12:3), circumcision was performed on the eighth day after birth, a custom that was retrojected into Abraham's life (Gen 17:10-14). The Palestinian Targum, that is, the Aramaic paraphrase and interpretation of the Hebrew Bible, reports an interesting, and very likely fictional, argument between Isaac and Ishmael. Isaac argues for his superiority over Ishmael because Isaac was circumcised, therefore pleasing to the Lord, at a very early age. Ishmael, acknowledging that he was circumcised at the age of thirteen, argues for his superiority over Isaac by noting that at puberty he could have resisted and rejected circumcision, but willingly accepted it. Who knows what Isaac would have done at puberty?

To appreciate the significance of circumcision and naming, it is important to recall the ancient understanding of conception. It was widely believed that the male deposited a fully formed miniature person in the woman who served merely as the "field" in which the "seed" would grow to maturity.

But women in the ancient Mediterranean world were considered to be lascivious and untrustworthy (read Sirach and Proverbs for illustrations of this concern). A husband never knew for sure whether the child born was actually his. Such uncertainty would weaken the family by making potential heirs suspect, thereby rendering the family treasure vulnerable to theft. So by circumcising and naming a boy as early as eight days after birth, the father made a public proclamation formally accepting this child as his son, no matter what other charges might be made later.

In Luke's Gospel, Joseph does not receive a "revelation" about Jesus and his divine origins, such as he does in Matthew's Gospel. Nevertheless, Joseph demonstrates that he is truly an honorable and just man by seeing to the circumcision and naming of his son in accord with the prescriptions of the Torah. Joseph's honorable behavior solidifies the bonds of his young family.

PURIFICATION OF MARY

Mary, too, shows herself to be a devout person who is eager to observe all the prescriptions of the Torah, including the obligation of her purification. (Notice Luke's ignorance of Palestinian custom by referring to "their" purification.)

By offering two doves at the purification rites instead of the preferred lamb, in obedience to Leviticus 12:6-8, Joseph and Mary reveal their social status. They very likely do not have the land on which to raise a lamb nor the ability to purchase one.

American believers tend to romanticize "the holy family." Too often it looks very much like a middle-class American family. Insights from Middle Eastern culture offer a healthy restraint to this tendency. Clearly, its deep faith and devout piety did not seem to spare this family its share of hardships and crises.

Epiphany
Matthew 2:1-12

Matthew alone reports this story about the Magi. No other ancient documents corroborate the account as actual, historical fact. Contemporary scholars believe that it was probably a preexisting tradition based on the Balaam story (Num 22–24) intending to demonstrate that Gentiles were part of God's plan from the very beginning. Scholars are divided, though, in their estimation of the degree of creativity exercised by the evangelist in shaping this story for his Gospel.

Mediterranean people, however, maintain a very porous boundary line between reality and appearance, fact and impressions. The appearance or impression is always considered much more significant than reality or the fact. This, of course, is all driven by that culture's overarching concern for honor, that is, public recognition and affirmation of proclaimed worth.

Joseph knows he is not the father of the child Mary is carrying (Matt 1:19). Matthew doesn't hide this fact. An angel of the Lord, a most honorable messenger from God, the source of all honor that counts, informs Joseph of the divinely willed circumstances of Jesus' conception and the function Jesus will play in God's plan: "He will save his people from their sins." But so far as we know, Joseph doesn't make this message public. He apparently lived with the secret all his life and presented a different impression to the public.

How can the evangelist give an honorable public appearance to the potentially embarrassing circumstances of Jesus' conception? Matthew begins Jesus' story with a genealogy, which in the ancient world is a key strategy for documenting one's claim to honor. Matthew does it cleverly with a number scheme based on David's name. Hebrew letters are also numbers, and the consonants DVD in Hebrew add up to fourteen. In this genealogy, Matthew clusters names in three groups of fourteen, more or less. The point: Jesus is none other than a descendent of David, Israel's greatest king!

Then Matthew reports the tradition about the Magi (not kings or astrologers) coming to pay homage to this descendant of royalty. A closer look at the story through the lenses of Mediterranean honor reveals how cleverly Matthew magnifies Jesus' honor rating.

KING OF JUDEANS

The Magi come seeking the newly born king of Judeans. Matthew and Matthew's Jesus during his ministry routinely identify God's people as "Israel" (see 2:6; also 8:10; 9:33; 10:6, 23; 15:24, 31; 19:28; 27:9). Three groups make up this people: "Judeans," "Galileans," and "Pereans." Outsiders ignored these distinctions and called everyone "Judeans" (the Greek word is often incorrectly translated "Jews"). Pilate calls Jesus of Nazareth in Galilee "King of the Judeans" (John 19:19-22).

Word that these visitors from the East are seeking a newly born king of Judeans strikes fear into the heart of old Herod who is the current, living king of Judeans. He knows that he has no newly born heir.

Then Matthew draws a contrast between these honorable visitors and the fearful ruler. Herod calls for the Magi "secretly" (v. 7). In the Middle East and all societies in which honor is the core value, privacy is a threat to honor. If honor is a public claim to worth along with a public acknowledgement of that worth, then people's behavior must be ever on public display. Anyone who acts secretly has something to hide and is therefore automatically considered to be dishonorable, shameful. Herod's secret inquiry immediately tags him as acting dishonorably.

The Magi listen to his request that they report to him what they find about this new king, but, astute Middle Easterners that they are, they refuse to enter into his shameful strategy.

They return home by a different route (v. 12), thereby deceiving the shameful Herod (Matt 2:16).

When the Magi find Jesus, they pay homage. The high, honorable status of these visitors indicates the high degree of honor they pay to Jesus and his mother. They also offer three kinds of gifts (gold, myrrh, and frankincense), further enhancing the honor they bestow. Matthew has masterfully cast Jesus into an impressively honorable context that does not fail to catch the attention of his original Middle Eastern audience.

Americans are familiar with pregnancy out of wedlock and the crisis this poses in a wide variety of social contexts. This formerly shameful experience was often hidden as best as possible from family and neighborhood. Things are different today. How would Matthew the evangelist present the predicament of Joseph, Mary, and Jesus if all of them were Americans?

Baptism of the Lord
Mark 1:7-11

Mark's brief account of Jesus' baptism is an excellent example of Scripture as "high context" literature which omits many important details because the author expects the listeners or readers to know them and fill in the gaps. In "low context" literature, no details are left out; examples are legal documents such as contracts, loan and credit card agreements, and mortgages.

Mark expected his audience to supply their distinctive cultural understanding of kinship, including paternity.

KINSHIP

Jesus presumably leaves his family and village to come to John for baptism. This movement is very symbolic. In the ancient Mediterranean world, family is one of the central social institutions. Individuals have no identity or meaningful existence apart from the family. Middle Eastern audiences would not miss the significance of Jesus' symbolic break with family ties. What will he do now? A person not embedded in a family is as good as dead. Jesus has taken what seems to be a very shameful step away from his family.

BAPTISM

The circumstances of the baptism of Jesus provide an immediate answer to this startling predicament. A voice emanating from the torn-open heavens declares Jesus to be son of God, beloved of and highly pleasing to the Father.

In the ancient world with its very primitive understanding of reproduction, it was impossible to prove who was the actual father of a child. For this reason, only when a father acknowledged a baby as his own did that boy or girl become a son or daughter.

We know that Joseph, by agreeing to marry Mary who was not pregnant by him, performed precisely this task on behalf of Jesus. Joseph accepted Jesus as his son and embedded him into the family to give him honorable standing and a secure setting in which to live.

Now that Jesus has symbolically left family and village behind, none other than God personally acknowledges him as a beloved and obedient son.

Still, one difficulty remains. Honor is a public proclamation of worth accompanied by a public acknowledgement of that worth. The torn heavens indicate that this is a public event. If not for that fact, Jesus' experience would be quite personal and, in this society, meaningless.

Yet the text does not mention crowds or other witnesses. Who else hears this statement? Who will acknowledge and confirm this public claim to honorable status for Jesus? Clearly, Mark expects those who hear and read the Gospel to recognize the eminent source of Jesus' honor and provide the confirmation required. You and I are expected to recognize Jesus as pleasing son of God.

Western readers generally find this story and discussion to be unengaging. Such communication between earthlings and supernatural, invisible beings is considered esoteric.

Yet the ancient Mediterranean world and many contemporary peasant societies maintain a strong belief in the reality of a spirit world which continually interacts with human beings. In Mark's Gospel, it is chiefly this spirit world that knows and acknowledges Jesus' identity as son of God. Here at the baptism, the divine voice is directed toward Jesus himself. When Jesus successfully challenges unclean spirits, they regularly acknowledge his honorable status and identity. They cry out: "holy one of God" (Mark 1:24); "son of God" (Mark 3:11); "son of the Most high God" (Mark 5:27). In Mark 9:7, God reveals to Jesus' core disciples (Peter, James, and John) his identity as "my son, my beloved." That this identity eventually became known but not accepted or believed by others is clear from the central charge against Jesus at his trial, that he claimed to be the Christ, "the son of the Blessed One" (Mark 14:61).

In the ancient Mediterranean world, Jesus' true identity was a critically important matter. A son of an artisan from a backwater village has no legitimacy as a public figure ("Where did this man get all this? . . . and they took offense at him" [Mark 6:2-3]). But the legitimacy of the son of God as a public figure is incontestable.

How do American believers "fill in the blanks" of high context passages in the Bible, such as Jesus' baptism?

Second Sunday in Ordinary Time
John 1:35-42

New Testament scholar Jerome Neyrey identifies an interesting pattern of missionary activity in the Gospel of John. Today's reading presents two of four successive examples.

THE PATTERN

(1) A believer in Jesus evangelizes another person (2) by using a special title of Jesus. (3) The evangelizer leads the convert to Jesus (4) who sees the newcomer and confirms his decision. (5) The conversion is sealed.

Example 1: John 1:35-39

(1) The Baptist evangelizes two of his own disciples (v. 35) (2) using the title "Lamb of God" (v. 36). (3) As a result, the two disciples followed Jesus (v. 37). (4) Jesus sees and invites them to "Come and see" (vv. 38-39). (5) They came, saw, and remained with him that day (v. 39), which was a Friday, or Sabbath eve (4 P.M.). This means the new converts stayed with Jesus until the Sabbath ended.

The Baptizer is a true herald of Jesus: "I myself have seen and have testified that this is the Son of God. . . . Look, here is the Lamb of God!" (John 1:34-35). He evangelizes two of his disciples who switch their allegiance from the Baptist to Jesus.

Example 2: John 1:40-43

One of these new converts is Andrew, the brother of Simon Peter. (1) Andrew goes to evangelize his brother, Simon Peter

(v. 40) (2) using the title "Messiah" (v. 41). (3) Andrew the evangelizer leads Simon Peter to Jesus (v. 42) (4) who looks at the newcomer and confirms him: "You are Cephas" (v. 42). (5) The sealing of Peter's conversion is not mentioned but known from the tradition.

Believers familiar with the Christian tradition are surprised to see Jesus change Peter's name here at the beginning of his ministry when in the Synoptic tradition that does not occur until later in the ministry (see Matt 16:18). Moreover, Andrew tells Peter now that Jesus is Messiah, and in the Synoptic tradition Peter doesn't seem to arrive at this conclusion until midway into the ministry (see Mark 8:29).

John the evangelist has compacted the development of discipleship into several striking scenes. In actuality, the process is longer, just as the Synoptic record indicates.

Example 3: John 1:43

In the case of Philip, the pattern seems truncated. The Greek text is not clear about exactly who found him: Peter or Andrew. Still, Jesus confirmed that conversion by inviting Philip to "follow me."

Example 4: John 1:45-50

(1) Philip evangelizes Nathanael about Jesus (v. 45) (2) describing him as "the one about whom Moses in the law and also the prophets wrote" (v. 45). (3) In reply to Nathanael's skepticism ("Can anything good come out of Nazareth?" v. 46), Philip invites Nathanael to meet Jesus: "Come and see." Nathanael stands out in this series as a difficult convert, not easily persuaded. (4) Jesus nevertheless confirms the conversion with the judgment: "Here is truly an Israelite in which there is no deceit!" (v. 47). (5) The conversion is sealed with Jesus' promise: "You will see greater things than these" (v. 50).

The missionary pattern is present in the story of the Samaritan woman as well. After being evangelized by Jesus, she in turn evangelizes the people of Sychar: "Come and see a man who told me everything I have ever done! He cannot be the Messiah, can he?" (John 4:29). They came, and saw, listened to Jesus, and ultimately became confirmed disciples (John 4:39-42).

The evangelist sets out a challenging pattern of evangelization. The first people to be evangelized preached Jesus in their turn to relatives, friends, and even to strangers.

The content of their preaching was essentially the "signs" of Jesus, and their aim was to get people to accept Jesus as a prophet or leader who bore the mark of God's approval. Sometimes the preachers based their activity on scriptural argument, as in the case of Philip and Nathanael.

Modern Christians are regularly exhorted to evangelize, but Americans find the task unpleasant and embarrassing. It conjures up images of pairs of evangelizers (Jehovah's witnesses, local Baptists, etc.), dressed in dark clothing, ringing doorbells throughout neighborhoods in search of converts.

These stereotyped figures seem to share one thing in common with the evangelizers in John: enthusiasm about Jesus. Where and how might contemporary believers discover and develop such enthusiasm?

Third Sunday in Ordinary Time
Mark 1:14-20

Today's reading from Mark presents a version of how Jesus recruited his first followers that differs from the version reported by John (see last Sunday's reflection).

JESUS AND THE BAPTIST

Scholars believe that after his baptism, Jesus became a disciple of John, preaching his message of repentance and baptizing others (see John 3:22). Over the course of time, Jesus began to discover a new ministry for himself. According to Mark, Jesus embarked upon it after John was arrested (v. 14).

The theme of Jesus' preaching is quite similar to that of the Baptist's: "the time is fulfilled, the kingdom of God has come near; repent, and believe in the good news" (v. 15). Jesus invites his listeners to give undivided loyalty to God whose definitive reign is about to begin.

JESUS RECRUITS HIS FACTION

Modern believers are amazed that the people Jesus invites to join him seem to drop everything and follow him immediately. It is all the more amazing if this is the first time they have met each other.

Cultural background and information shed light on the story. It is highly likely that Jesus and the four followers he summons here are not strangers. If they have not personally met each other before this time, they were aware of each other's aspirations and objectives. News travelled quickly in the ancient world thanks to gossip networks.

Jesus the artisan moves from Nazareth, an insignificant village, to Capernaum, a hub of activity on the Sea of Galilee at the crossroads of major highways. His presence and activity stir curiosity and become the topic of gossip. He does not seem to have gone there to seek work. Instead, he appears to be seeking people to join him in a common venture.

Gathering a following is a common occurrence in the Mediterranean world. Technically, a group that gathers for a specific purpose for a limited time is called a "coalition." The coalition that Jesus gathers is technically called a "faction" because it focuses on a central person who holds and controls the loyalty of the group. Invariably, the faction leader has a grievance and gathers around him others who share the grievance.

What were the grievance and the aspirations, objectives, and hopes of the fishermen who joined Jesus' faction? These are never spelled out. The facts, however, that Jesus was known as the son of an artisan and that these first four members of his group were fishermen make it probable that they found common cause in the oppressive difficulties of their daily lives. Such experiences would be the underpinning for Jesus' broader project of proclaiming the reign of God, the authentic patron or father of Israel.

In societies where central government is weak, people develop more reliable ways of meeting their needs. Patronage is such a system in the Mediterranean world. People with means (patrons) are expected to help those will less or no means (clients). Many refused to play the role of patron (Luke 12:15-21) prompting Jesus to point to God as the only reliable patron for Israel.

Fishing was a major industry in the first century, much too demanding to be the pastime of a single family. The brothers Simon and Andrew worked with their father Jonah, while the brothers James and John worked with their father Zebedee. These two families very likely formed a corporation that also employed "hired hands" (v. 20), that is, day laborers.

Such corporations were contracted to provide fish in return for payment in cash or in processed fish. First-century records indicate the payment was frequently irregular and inadequate.

Moreover, fishing was part of the tax network. Toll collectors, like Matthew, leased fishing rights to corporations in return for a percentage of the catch, sometimes as high as 40 percent.

Jonah and Zebedee had to hire more day laborers to replace their sons who followed Jesus. They calculated that this short-term gamble might improve their lot if Jesus could deliver what he promised.

Western believers like to romanticize Jesus' call of his first followers. Cultural insights demonstrate that issues of livelihood were at stake. What real-life issues in America prompt people to follow Jesus with undivided loyalty?

Fourth Sunday
in Ordinary Time
Mark 1:21-28

Middle Eastern cultures and indeed a large part of the ancient and modern world believe in spirits, good and bad. The
West has allowed science and particularly the medical sci-
ences to explain instances of "human beings possessed by
spirits" in a different way. This makes the present story difficult for Westerners to accept and appreciate. From a Middle
Eastern perspective, the meaning of the story is very plain.

JESUS THE ARTISAN WHO TEACHES

It is not the unclean spirit and the possessed man that
trouble Jesus' audience. These were common in their world.
They are disturbed because Jesus is acting totally out of line
with his inherited status. This artisan from Nazareth dares to
teach "as one having authority" in the Capernaum synagogue.
Who gave him authority to teach?

JESUS THE TEACHER WITH POWER OVER SPIRITS

As the listeners puzzle over Jesus' behavior, his teaching, and
his manner of teaching, a man possessed by an unclean spirit
interrupts the setting by shrieking.

Our ancestors in the faith believed that spirits were more
powerful than human beings but less powerful than God.

Spirits readily interfered (or intervened) in human life, sometimes benevolently, sometimes capriciously, and sometimes malevolently. They had power to control human behavior.

The spirit who possessed the man in the synagogue is central in this story because he knows Jesus' identity far better than Jesus' compatriots do. He knows Jesus is "the Holy one of God."

According to ancient magical practice, one means of protection against the power of malicious or malevolent spirits is to call out the name (and true identity) of that spirit. The apocryphal *Testament of Solomon* is like a modern-day physician's desk reference listing the names of various spirits, what they do, and how human beings might thwart or counteract their power. For instance, "The nineteenth [spirit] said, 'I am called Mardero. I inflict incurable fevers; write my name in some such way in the house, and I retreat immediately'" (*Testament of Solomon* 18.23). By shouting out Jesus' true identity, the unclean spirit seeks to thwart Jesus' power.

But much to the amazement of the people, Jesus is not controlled or cowed by this unclean spirit. Instead, Jesus shows that his power is stronger than that of the spirit. Jesus commands the spirit to come out of the man, and it does!

The people now have an answer to why Jesus teaches "with authority, and not as the scribes." Clearly, Jesus possesses powers stronger than those of ordinary human beings. Some Greek manuscripts have variant readings of the people's response to Jesus in Mark 1:27: "What is this? A new teaching? With authority he commands even the unclean spirits, and they obey him."

Authority is a major problem for Jesus' contemporaries. No one denies the mighty deeds of power that Jesus performs. What troubles them is the source of his authority. Is it God? (Mark, of course, has already told this to his listeners and readers a number of times.) Or is it the world of the other, lesser gods and spirits?

The people in the synagogue at Capernaum have not yet decided. The fact, however, is very clear. Jesus the artisan from Nazareth has authority and effective power to do what he does. He behaves not shamefully, out of alignment with his status, but rather quite honorably. And this is why Mark concludes by noting: "At once his reputation [honor] began to spread throughout the surrounding region of Galilee."

This final note affects the honor of both Jesus and the healed man. The gossip network proclaims a new honor status for Jesus (teaches with authority; has power over unclean spirits) that contrasts with his status "of Nazareth." It also restores honor to the man now released from the power of unclean spirits. He can reclaim his rightful place in the community.

The Western tendency to rationalize the ancient understanding of spirits is rooted in the fact that Westerners have much more power over their lives and circumstances than the ancients believed they had. Today's reflection invites Westerners to consider how wisely or imprudently they use their power.

Fifth Sunday in Ordinary Time
Mark 1:29-39

Modern Western readers of the Bible are ever curious about the health problems Jesus appears to have addressed effectively. The fever experienced by Peter's mother-in-law, the people afflicted with demons, the "various diseases" (v. 35) presented to Jesus all raise a host of questions. The basic questions are, what really happened? did Jesus really do it?

Contemporary medical anthropologists offer some helpful insights. They distinguish between disease as a biomedical malfunction that afflicts an organism, and illness as a disvalued human condition in which social networks are ruptured and life's meaning is lost. Curing is aimed at disease; it is a rare occurrence. Healing is aimed at illness; it occurs infallibly all the time for all people. Everyone works out a new meaning in life no matter what the predicament.

It is nearly impossible for us to know what diseases afflicted the people who came to Jesus for help. But the texts do reveal the social consequences of their affliction and how Jesus remedied those consequences as well as the affliction, whatever it was. Consider Peter's mother-in-law.

PETER'S HOUSE

The ideal marriage partner in the ancient Mediterranean world is a first cousin, specifically, the young man's father's brother's daughter. Moreover, the wife always moves into the husband's household, for the sons continue to live with their father even after marriage. But they have a place of their own in an often large housing complex.

Peter's mother-in-law, the wife of his father's brother, should be living in her husband's house. If he has died, she should be living with one of the sons, or if they have died she would return to her family. That she is in Peter's house suggests that she may have no living family members to take care of her. In the Middle Eastern world, this is a fate worse than any sickness, indeed, worse than death. As often happens in Jesus' ministry, the challenge is more than the woman's fever.

JESUS THE FOLK HEALER

In the ancient world, professional physicians did not attempt to heal people. If they failed, they could be put to death. They preferred to talk about illnesses, after the fashion of philosopher-physicians. These are the physicians to whom the New Testament refers when it (infrequently) uses that word (Mark 2:17; 5:26; Luke 4:23; 8:43; Col 4:14).

Folk healers were more abundant and were much more willing to use their hands and risk a failed treatment. Peasants had easy access to such healers and resorted to them frequently. In the Gospels, Jesus is portrayed as a folk healer: a spirit-filled prophet and teacher who has power over unclean spirits and a wide variety of illness.

One very consistent element in Jesus' healing activity is that he restores sick persons to their proper status, role, and place in the community. Lepers declared cleansed rejoin the holy community of God. The dead restored to life return to membership in their family.

In today's gospel reading, Jesus takes Peter's mother-in-law by the hand and helps her up. Anyone familiar with Mediterranean culture knows that they are more willing to touch each other than germ-obsessed Americans. They stand closer to each other when they speak, and they frequently touch. It is not Jesus' simple touch that is important; his touch mediates his power. On another occasion, a woman who touched only his cloak drew upon his power without his knowing it, and she was healed (Mark 5:30).

That Peter's mother-in-law immediately began to serve Jesus and his disciples demonstrates that Jesus has really healed her. She is strong enough to resume her status, role, and normal function in the home. Jesus has restored meaning to her life. In typical Mediterranean fashion, she reciprocates the favor by serving him and those with him.

The teaching and healing ministry of Jesus challenge America's continuing efforts to reform its health care delivery system. Above all, people need meaning in life. That's what healing is about.

Sixth Sunday in Ordinary Time
Mark 1:40-45

In 1868, the Norwegian scientist Gerhard Hansen discovered the biomedical cause of leprosy, an extremely chronic but not very infectious disease. Spouses rarely contract it from their infected partners. Basically it causes a loss of sensation and a progressive though painless ulceration of the extremities. Facial nodules develop, but leprosy very rarely affects the scalp. It is never white in color.

On the basis of this and even more detailed scientific knowledge, scholars are quite certain that biblical leprosy such as discussed in Leviticus 13–14 and in today's gospel is not modern leprosy. Even the Hebrew and Greek words used in the Bible are not the proper words for "real" leprosy.

What then is the concern? and what did Jesus do?

THE CONCERN

In Leviticus, it is quite definite that our ancestors in the faith are describing a repulsive, scaly condition. When it affected the skin, modern scientists think it may have been something like psoriasis. It was a real experience, but it was not modern leprosy.

Leviticus 13–14 notes that even clothes and the walls of homes can suffer from it. The significance of the descriptions baffles modern readers, but it clearly meant something serious to the ancients.

Our ancestors in the faith were mindful of the divine command to "be holy as the Lord your God is holy" (Lev 19:2) Holiness encompassed many qualities, not the least important of which was bodily wholeness and integrity. Anyone with physical imperfections was clearly not holy as the Lord is holy. "For no one who has a blemish may draw near, a man blind or lame, or one who has a mutilated face or a limb too long, or a man with an injured foot or an injured hand, or a hunchback, or a dwarf, or a man with a defect in his sight or an itching disease or scabs or crushed testicles" (Lev 21:16-20). None of these can approach the Lord. Leviticus commands that the person afflicted with "biblical" leprosy must "live alone; his dwelling shall be outside the camp" (Lev 13:46).

It is impossible to underestimate the impact of this judgment. Mediterranean cultures are gregarious and group-oriented. They need community to live just as a fish needs water. Without community, social network, connections and relations with others, the other-directed Mediterranean person suffers and can die from seclusion.

JESUS HEALS THE LEPER

Moved with compassion, Jesus came to the petitioner's rescue. Notice that Jesus' command is in the passive voice: "Be made clean." In biblical literature this is known as the theological or divine passive, that is, it acknowledges God as the one who performs the action without having to use God's name. Jesus willed it; God cleanses the leper.

It is impossible to say what really happened. Did the problem disappear on the spot? Was the condition "debatable," such that Jesus could look at it and say it was not there, while the priests in the Temple might look at it and say it still was there?

What is of much greater import in Jesus' behavior is that he touched the man. While touching is common in this culture, touching a leper is not. Remember, "modern" leprosy is minimally "catchy." The ancients surely knew this of that scaly skin condition as well. The concern of the ancients was not that the situation was "catchy," but that it was "dirty": not infectious, but polluting. People who had the problem

did not infect the community; they polluted it. For this reason, they had to live outside the camp, apart from God's holy
people, alone, until the pollution was gone.

By touching the "leper" Jesus challenges his culture's judgment. In Jesus' view, the "leper's" problem is not polluting,
and with his touch he restores the leper to full membership
in God's community, to solidarity in human fellowship.

The ancient distinction between an infecting and a polluting condition is worth pondering. The consequences are very
different, too. Can you identify parallel or comparable situations in contemporary society? How should a Christian respond to them?

Seventh Sunday in Ordinary Time
Mark 2:1-12

WANDERING NEWSPAPERS

In the Mediterranean world, everybody minds everybody else's business. Verse 1 signals the effectiveness of the gossip network which spread the news that Jesus was at home. In the ancient world, women were the primary purveyors of community news, assisted by young boys and girls who could wander freely through other households to snoop on adults and report back (see 1 Tim 3:11 and compare 2 Tim 3:6-7). Because of the power of such information, women played a key role in controlling the social behavior of the community.

GROUP-ORIENTATION

The entire story resonates with indications of the group-centered character of Mediterranean culture. Notice that the paralytic was brought to Jesus by a group and carried by four men (v. 3). This is not just camaraderie but customary, strong Mediterranean social cohesiveness. In fact, it is the loyalty of this group to Jesus that moves him to heal the paralytic (v. 5).

The Greek word ordinarily translated "faith" is more appropriately translated "loyalty." It describes people who pledge themselves to another person "no matter what." This group was well aware of the hostile scribes who sat in Jesus' home watching him carefully (v. 6). That didn't deter them from publicly demonstrating their loyalty to Jesus.

PARALYSIS

Leviticus (21:16-24) specifies that among other physically challenged people, a lame person may not approach to offer the bread of his God (see also Deut 23:1-2). To our ancestors in the faith, the physical condition itself was not as serious as the social consequences: exclusion from God's holy community.

In today's episode, Jesus phrased it thus: "Which is easier, to say to the paralytic, 'Your sins are forgiven' [repairing the social condition], or to say 'Rise, take up your mat and walk' [repairing the physical condition; v 9]?" Clearly his culture sees restoration to normal functioning as easier to achieve than restoring someone to full membership in the community.

HEALING

Recall the distinction between disease and illness offered by medical anthropology (see Fifth Sunday above). Sickness, one among many misfortunes in human life, can be viewed as disease or illness. The disease view focuses on causes of sickness from a scientific, biomedical perspective. It looks for germs, viruses, and the like and seeks to find the "silver bullet" (penicillin, radiation, chemotherapy) that will destroy the cause and restore health. The illness view focuses on social consequences of a sickness event, both for the sick and for family and community.

The process of conquering a disease is known as curing; the process of restoring meaning to the life of a sick person and that person's family and community is known as healing. Modern science admits that cures are rare, but healing takes place always, for everyone, all the time. Everyone ultimately finds meaning in life.

Jesus first *heals* the paralytic by pronouncing that God forgives his sin and wants to revive their mutual, intimate relationship: "Your sins are forgiven!" (v. 5). By addressing this man as "son," Jesus publicly announces that the man is now a member of Jesus' fictive-kinship group, his own family-like community.

When Jesus perceives that the scribes grumble because he acts like a broker on behalf of God, who alone forgives sins

(v. 8), he takes yet a further step. He cures the man's disability: "Take up your mat and go home!" (v. 11). Even here, Jesus demonstrates his primary interest in healing. By telling him to "go home," Jesus restores the man to his own community. Regaining full membership in his community and finding welcome in Jesus' community truly restores meaning to this group-oriented man's life. He is definitely healed.

By mentioning the man's mat (vv. 9, 11-12), Mark indicates the social status of the man or of his community: poor. Matthew and Luke raise the social status by replacing mat with "bed." In either case, the commitment of the entire ancient Mediterranean community to caring about the health and well-being of all its members—poor and rich—is a stirring challenge to individualistic Western believers. We must indeed be our sisters' and brothers' keepers.

Eighth Sunday in Ordinary Time
Mark 2:18-22

Like many other familiar ideas in the Bible, fasting in the ancient Mediterranean world is a very different practice from contemporary fasting.

FASTING

The only fasting prescribed in the Law of Moses is associated with the Day of Atonement (see Lev 16:3-28; 23:26-32; 25:9; Num 29:7-11; Exod 30:10). The key Hebrew phrase in these passages translated "afflict yourselves" literally means "bow down your soul." Psalm 35:13 connects the phrase with fasting: "I afflicted myself with fasting." By New Testament times, fasting was so closely associated with the Day of Atonement that the feast was called simply "the fast day" (Acts 27:9; Josephus *Antiquities* 3.10.3).

A review of the occurrences of these Hebrew words and phrases reveals that the key idea associated with fasting and afflicting oneself is self-humiliation. Indeed the Hebrew word that describes fasting rituals is *ta'anit,* that is, humiliation.

FASTING AS SELF-HUMILIATION

A person who fasts refuses to eat or drink or sometimes even to engage in sexual relations (see 2 Sam 12:16-24). Like everything else in the Mediterranean world, so too is fasting a very public event. One fasts in the presence of one's fellow citizens and, of course, God. The purpose of this kind of public self-humiliation is to move others to action. The one fasting is begging for assistance from others without ever saying so explicitly in words. Fasting speaks louder than words.

FASTING IN JESUS' TIME

The fasting required on the Day of Atonement was intended to move God to forgive the sins of those fasting. The idea was that if human beings can be effectively moved to compassion and practical assistance by the self-humiliation of a needy person caught in a crisis, how much more promptly should God act when faced with fasting.

The Pharisees established a custom of fasting twice a week (see Luke 18:12), on Mondays and Thursdays. Matthew's report (6:16-18) suggests that some Pharisees fasted not because they were needy but rather to impress others with their asceticism. They used make-up to look gaunt, making sure no one could miss the fact that they were fasting. Jesus compared them to actors (the Greek word translated "hypocrites" literally means "actor").

Today's gospel states that John's disciples were also fasting. Since John preached a "baptism of repentance for the forgiveness of sin" (Mark 1:4), he and his disciples humiliated themselves with fasting (and he in addition with his camel's hair garb) to move the populace to heed their warnings. People were urged to prepare themselves for the coming of one mightier than John (Mark 1:7) who would claim: "Yahweh-God is about to intervene on behalf of his people-in-crisis [Roman occupation]. Place your unswerving loyalty in him!" (Mark 1:14-15).

JESUS AND COMPANY DO NOT FAST

Jesus began his ministry as a disciple of John, but after John's imprisonment Jesus struck out on his own (Mark 1:14). He gathered his own disciples (Mark 1:16-20) and embarked on a healing ministry (Mark 1:21–2:12).

Jesus' successes in his ministry, so different from John's, persuade him God indeed is already rescuing his people. If this is so, there is no need of self-humiliation to persuade God to act.

This, in effect, is what Jesus says to those who ask why he and his disciples are not fasting. Jesus compares himself to a bridegroom and his followers to guests at the wedding feast. It would be a serious insult and an indication that they did not approve of the wedding if guests refused to enjoy fully the celebration (e.g., if they fasted).

To drive his point home, Mark's Jesus concludes with another parable highlighting that something very new is happening. New wine must be put in new wineskins. Old wineskins may not be able to withstand the creative pressures of the new vintage.

Though fasting does not carry the same meaning in the modern Western world as it did in the ancient Mediterranean, human beings continue to suffer severe crises and overwhelming evil. Americans cry for help out of their humbling experiences of unemployment, loss of health benefits, loss of home, and more. Cultural analysts observe, however, that Americans are moved more by crises televised from halfway around the world than by tragedy on their doorsteps.

Ninth Sunday
in Ordinary Time
Mark 2:23–3:6

SABBATH

The Gospels record that it was Jesus' custom to attend synagogue on the Sabbath (Mark 1:21, 29; see Luke 4:16). They
also report that he provoked conflict by his behavior on the
Sabbath.

Already in Mark's Gospel, it was on the Sabbath that Jesus
cast an unclean spirit out of a man in the synagogue (1:21-
28) and healed Peter's mother-in-law (1:29-30). In today's
reports, it is again a Sabbath when Jesus and his disciples
pluck and eat ears of grain, and Jesus heals another man in
the synagogue (2:18–3:6).

On the one hand, it is clear that the Pharisees and other
authorities perceive Jesus as challenging their traditional interpretation of Sabbath obligations. On the other hand, Mark's
Jesus claims authority ("the Son of man is lord of the sabbath," v. 28) to reinterpret the Sabbath or restore its original
understanding ("the sabbath was made for humankind, and
not humankind for the sabbath," v. 27).

HONOR

In the larger picture, something even more serious is going
on. Jesus is winning every hostile encounter with his opponents. This is bound to have serious repercussions.

Honor is a public claim to worth and a public recognition of that worth. In the Gospels, the Pharisees never miss an opportunity to claim their share of honor. Experts on proper religious behavior and minute observance of the Torah, they tallied 613 commandments that obligated every member of the Judaic religion. Many Pharisees took special pride in observing all the commandments (see Luke 18:9-12).

Yet each time they challenge Jesus with a question, he shuts them up with his response. The episode in the cornfield is particularly interesting. The Pharisees challenge Jesus by pointing out that his disciples are doing something unlawful on the Sabbath (v. 24).

Jesus refers them to the Scripture they claim to know so well. As usual, he begins with an insult: "Have you never *read . . .* " (v. 25). Only 2 to 4 percent of the populace was literate, but experts in the Law were very likely in that elite group. When dealing with the illiterate peasantry, Jesus is very careful to ask: "Have you never *heard . . .* ?"

Then Jesus reminds the Pharisees of a story they surely read concerning the time David entered the house of God and ate the bread intended only for the priests, at the time when "Abiathar" was high priest. This is erroneous. The incident is recorded in 1 Samuel 21:1-6 where the high priest is Ahimelech. Abiathar was high priest at a much later point in David's career, after he became king (2 Sam 15:32-37).

Who made the mistake? If Mark or an earlier tradition recorded an erroneous recollection, some scribe would have "corrected" it in a subsequent manuscript. (For instance, John 4:2 is a scribal "correction" of John 3:22.) But the manuscript evidence indicates that Abiathar was the name reported consistently in this passage of Mark's Gospel.

Did Jesus make the mistake? If he did, someone among these scholars should and would have pounced on it. No one did! If Jesus made the mistake intentionally, then the report indicates that he had the last laugh at these experts. Perhaps Mark didn't record that part of the exchange in which Jesus revealed how he tripped them up at their own game. No matter. The Scripture-savvy reader knows that Jesus has beaten these Scripture experts at their own game.

THE PENALTY FOR CAUSING SHAME

However one might resolve the grain field episode, it is not difficult to appreciate the cumulative effect of being beaten in games of honor. "The Pharisees went out, and immediately held counsel with the Herodians against him, how to destroy him" (Mark 3:6). In the Mediterranean world, honor is a matter of life and death.

Americans, especially those whose ethnic heritage does not derive from a circum-Mediterranean culture, have enormous difficulty appreciating the pivotal importance of honor in these cultures. During the Persian Gulf crisis, American leaders mistakenly insisted that honor did not enter the picture. In the Middle East, honor permeates all of life.

Americans have a difficult time understanding that Jesus' consummate ability to shame his opponents contributed to his death. In modern-day America, it would have contributed to his wealth.

Tenth Sunday in Ordinary Time
Mark 3:20-35

NAMING

"Sticks and stones will break my bones, but names will never hurt me." American youngsters often repeat this piece of street wisdom during name-calling disputes with their peers. That someone may ultimately break into tears and flee or decide to retaliate with physical force suggests that the saying reflects wishful thinking more than actual reality.

In the ancient Mediterranean world, calling people names was a key strategy for honoring or shaming them. Honorable titles applied to Jesus include "Holy One of God" (Mark 1:24), "bridegroom" (Mark 2:19-20), "Son of God" (Mark 3:11), "the Messiah" (Mark 8:29), among others.

Today's episode records phrases intended to shame and discredit Jesus: "beside himself" (= crazy, from his "relatives"!), "possessed by Beelzebub," "acts by the power of the prince of demons," "has an unclean spirit." If such descriptions can be made to stick, Jesus' career is ended. The purpose of these labels is to identify him as deviant, as failing to measure up and stick to his honor status, which derives from birth. Names can "break bones" and end life in this culture.

The response of his relatives is significant. A Western reader might wonder: "Relatives call him crazy? With relatives like that who needs enemies?" Actually, declaration of insanity is a legitimate cultural ploy for protecting the life of one who deserved death. It also helped maintain the honor of the family in which the serious shame originated.

Earlier in Mark's story line, Jesus so infuriated the Pharisees that they plotted with the Herodians to destroy him (Mark 3:6). Honor and shame are very public matters in the Mediterranean world. If the shame is particularly egregious it can require the death of the one who caused it. For example, a rapist deserved death (see 2 Sam 13), but his life could be spared if the family declared him crazy. Even so, he would never be able to participate fully in the life of the community and would be culturally dead though physically alive.

Jesus prefers to defend himself. He has already demonstrated superb skill in challenge and riposte and is about to do it again. First he denies the charge (vv. 23-26). Jesus is Satan's foe and not his servant. Jesus' ministry snatches victims back from Satan's dominion.

Second, Jesus' ministry of healing and exorcism is a boon and not a bane to his clients. The only one hurt is Satan whom Jesus has effectively restrained ("he first binds the strong man," v. 27).

Third, Jesus aligns himself with God, a higher and more powerful authority than Satan in the hierarchy of the spirit world (vv. 28-30). The word "spirit" means power, activity, behavior, the ability to perform or do things. The word "holy" identifies the source of this power, namely God. Jesus functions by the power of God and not the power of Satan.

Whoever denies this claim, which is what Jesus' opponents are doing, severs any possible connection with God. This is what the Greek word "blasphemy" entails. Literally, the word means to shame another person by outrageous verbal insult. Denying God's activity and attributing it to an evil spirit insults God.

Earlier (Mark 2:1-12), Jesus' opponents accused him of blaspheming by claiming to act on God's behalf in forgiving sin. It was this and not his healing and exorcism that so disturbed his opponents that they plotted to kill him (3:6). Now Jesus turns the charge of blasphemy right back at his opponents. By denying that divine forgiveness is accessible through Jesus they insult God outrageously, cut themselves off from the source of forgiveness, and seal their own destruction.

Once again, Jesus wins a game of challenge and riposte. His honor increases; his reputation spreads.

The concluding segment of today's gospel reports Jesus' reaction to the efforts of his relatives (including his mother and brothers, v. 31) to spare his life by declaring him crazy (v. 21). The harsh tone of Jesus' question: "Who are my mother and my brothers?" indicates that Jesus did not appreciate their earlier efforts on his behalf. In a truly startling move, Jesus redefines family. More valuable than bonds of flesh and blood is ready obedience to the will of God. Such people constitute Jesus' new family.

It is impossible to exaggerate the importance of honor in the cultural world of Jesus. What value or values in the United States would stir similar passions? Would wealth be among them?

First Sunday of Lent
Mark 1:12-15

THE TEST OF HONOR

Since scholars recognize Mark's as the earliest of the Gospels, his simple version of the Temptation of Jesus is also considered the primitive report which Matthew and Luke embellished by creating three specific temptations.

From the Mediterranean cultural perspective, the temptation of Jesus by Satan is inevitable after the honorable tribute by the voice from heaven: "You are my Son, the Beloved; with you I am well pleased" (Mark 1:11). Every claim to honor is sure to be tested. Someone will try to prove that the compliment was false.

Though Mark does not report Jesus' response to the testing, the reader can assume that Jesus successfully defends his honor as pleasing and beloved Son. Remember that the opening verse of this Gospel established Jesus' claim to honor: "The beginning of the proclamation of Jesus the Messiah, the Son of God" (1:1).

Then we note that Jesus left his kinship network in Nazareth of Galilee to meet with John in the wilderness (Mark 1:9) where Jesus subsequently finds himself apparently alone with Satan (v. 13). The Mediterranean reader realizes that without his kinship network, Jesus is particularly vulnerable to attack by anyone and everyone. The Mediterranean reader is quite frightened for Jesus until reminded that "the angels waited on him" (v. 13). Of course! The Son of God has a different kinship network which does not abandon him. With such help,

Jesus certainly defended his honor successfully against Satan's tests.

JESUS AND JOHN

Perhaps because of the brevity of Mark's account of the temptation, the gospel selection for this cycle includes the subsequent verses which describe how Jesus initiates his ministry.

Scholars believe that Mark has skipped over a bit of "history" between verses 13 and 14. After his baptism by John, Jesus very likely became John's disciple and baptized others into his baptism (see John 3:22 and contrast the "corrective" in John 4:2). The similarity of Jesus' proclamation ("repent and believe in the good news," v. 15) to John's preaching of a "baptism of repentance for the forgiveness of sins" (Mark 1:3) strongly suggests that the initial relationship between Jesus and John was that of disciple and leader. Even so, the basic message is: the reign of God is imminent. Here is where the listeners must place their loyalty.

When John was arrested, Jesus and others who followed John were left without a leader. In the Mediterranean world where groups are a central feature of life, and rugged individualism is entirely foreign, the loss of a faction leader is a shocking experience.

In the meantime, as the references in John's Gospel make clear, Jesus attracted followers to himself. This puzzled the Baptist (see Luke 7:18-23) and some of his followers. Jesus' growing experience of success in healing and exorcism persuaded him to undertake a separate ministry, and John's arrest was the appropriate time to begin.

Mark summarizes and simplifies this development: Jesus was baptized by John and successfully defended his honor against Satan. When John was arrested, Jesus initiated his ministry, and only then went about recruiting followers for his faction. Such behavior is perfectly honorable, as one would expect from none other than the Son of God.

While Matthew's and Luke's accounts of the temptation provide an opportunity for Christians to ponder the three tests on the First Sunday of Lent in cycles A and C, Mark's account offers a different consideration. The preaching of

John echoed by Jesus invites all believers to consider where they place their loyalty. The Greek word translated as "faith" ("believe in the good news") can be translated culturally by "loyalty," that is, the social glue that binds people together in Mediterranean society.

Loyalty, commitment, solidarity–this is the cluster of values that Jesus invites his followers to embrace. Primarily, of course, these values should be directed to the God of Israel, whether in the midst of a storm (Mark 4:40), when seeking a healing from Jesus, God's prophet (Mark 5:34:10:52), or at any other time. Jesus himself is praised for his loyalty (Heb 3:1-3) and obedience to God (Heb 5:8). Mark would very likely second Matthew's challenge: "stay loyal to God and do not hesitate in your loyalty" (21:21).

Second Sunday of Lent
Mark 9:2-10

The story of Jesus' "transfiguration" is more appropriately described by the technical term "theophany," that is, an appearance of God to an individual person. The Bible reports a number of theophanies, the most notable being those experienced by Moses (Exod 19–20; 34) and Elijah (1 Kgs 19:4-18).

The appearance of God to Jesus reported by Mark includes elements that are common to all these accounts. *(1) Mountain.* The setting for the appearance is customarily a mountain (Mark 9:2b; Sinai for Moses; Horeb for Elijah). *(2) Witnesses.* Frequently there are "eyewitnesses" to the event (9:2a), though they may not see and hear exactly the same things experienced by the one to whom God is appearing. *(3) Signs.* The witnesses or the accounts report visible signs that the event is occurring. Jesus was "transfigured before them" (v. 2c); "his garments glistening, intensely white" (v. 3a); "a cloud overshadowed them, and from the cloud there came a voice" (v. 7). *(4) Shared experience.* The witnesses sometimes share in the experience. Peter, James, and John see Moses and Elijah conversing with Jesus (v. 4).

It is not clear whether the disciples heard intelligible conversation between Jesus and the prophets, or whether they heard the statement of the heavenly voice. At the end, Jesus forbids them to tell what they had seen (v. 9) but says nothing about what they had heard. Only Matthew (17:9) calls the event a "vision."

FUNCTION

Scholars in general agree on the function of this experience: God commissions the recipient of the theophany to some new role and status. The Baptism of Jesus was a theophany in which Jesus was authorized by God to preach and perform mighty deeds (Mark 1:15–8:30). At the midpoint in Mark's Gospel, the transfiguration is a theophany that authorizes Jesus to make his way to Jerusalem to meet his destiny, the cross, and his vindication (Mark 8:31–16:8). Clearly, theophanies involve revelation.

NATURE

There is less agreement on the nature of the experience. Some have interpreted the transfiguration as a resurrection appearance retrojected into Jesus' life, but this opinion is not well supported and is generally rejected.

Recent commentators interpret the transfiguration as a prophecy of Jesus' parousia, that is, something like a prelude or foreshadowing of Jesus' future coming in glory as judge. We might term this a "preview of coming attractions." Still others call it "eschatological" without explaining in plain English exactly what that means.

ALTERNATE REALITY

There is a much simpler explanation for the nature of the event. The technical description is "an experience of alternate reality," or an altered state of consciousness. Anthropologists note that such experiences are universal human phenomena, experienced in a wide variety of forms by all human beings. Ninety percent of 488 societies from all parts of the world studied by scientists routinely had this kind of experience. Anthropologist Erika Bourguignon concludes that "societies which *do not* utilize these states clearly are historical exceptions to be explained, rather than the vast majority of societies that do use these states."

In a fifth-century document, *The Sayings of the Fathers* (PG 64:314c-d), an anecdote describes the visit of a pagan priest to a monastery at Scetis to observe the life of the monks. He asked whether as a result of their lifestyle "you see anything of your God?" The abbot Olympius said no. The pagan priest said when he and his fellow priests lived the same lifestyle, "[our God] hides nothing from us but reveals his mysteries to us." He wondered if the monks were putting an obstacle in God's way. The elders told the abbot they agreed with the priest's observation.

Physician and anthropologist Arthur Kleinman would agree. He observes that the modern, secular West has been particularly effective in blocking access to these pan-human dimensions of the self. The human potential is still there and can be developed, though scientifically oriented Westerners seem fearful of anything over which they cannot exert complete control.

Viewing the story of Jesus' transfiguration as an experience of God commonly available in more than 90 percent of the world's cultures presents an exciting new challenge to Western Christians this Lenten season. The Advent prayer, "Come Lord Jesus," inspires a new Lenten prayer: "Lord God, help me to see you face to face as did Moses (Deut 34:10) and Jesus (Mark 9) and many other of your servants through the course of history even to this day."

Third Sunday of Lent
John 2:13-25

Those who follow the Church's guidelines and apply historical-critical methods in interpreting the Bible expect to discover more than one layer of tradition in various texts. In today's gospel, the word "remembered" or "recalled" (see vv. 17 and 22) is a technical term used by John to describe the process by which the community of believers gradually came to view Jesus as the fulfillment of Scripture after his resurrection. Thus, verses 17 and 22 do not describe on-the-spot responses of Jesus' immediate followers but rather the evangelist's interpretation of the event more than sixty years after the fact.

PROPHETIC ACTION

Jesus' "cleansing of the Temple" is the obvious "historical" event that John describes. All the evangelists report it, but the Synoptics place it just prior to Jesus' trial, making it the more proximate cause of Jesus' death. John locates it much earlier in the ministry because he has made the raising of Lazarus from the dead the more proximate cause of Jesus' death. Scholars think the Synoptic version is historically more likely.

Granting that this is a historical event, how did Jesus' contemporaries perceive and interpret what he was doing and saying? Roman denarii and Attic drachmas bore pagan or imperial portraits and were unacceptable in paying the Temple tax (see Matt 17:27). Moneychangers performed a necessary service by exchanging these coins for acceptable coins of Tyre.

Animals, too, were necessary for sacrifice, but it seems the danger of an escaped animal entering the holy of holies was a risk originally avoided by keeping them outside the Temple precincts. It was likely Caiaphas who introduced them into the Temple precincts.

If Jesus' contemporaries perceived abuses or potential abuses in these two activities, then Jesus the prophet is clearly viewed as performing a "prophetic symbolic action" after the fashion of Jeremiah (7:11) and Ezekiel. Such an action actually sets in motion the judgment spoken by the prophet. "Stop making the house of my Father a house of marketing!"

BODY AND COMMUNITY

The second historical question in this scene concerns Jesus' authority. "What sign can you show us for doing this?" This is a legitimate concern for those responsible for proper Temple behavior. Jesus' answer, however, is totally unintelligible in historical context. In fact it is absurd. "Destroy this temple and in three days I will raise it up." The actual historical reconstruction of the Temple was begun by Herod the Great around 20 B.C.E. and completed around 62 C.E.

Jesus' original audience would have interpreted Jesus' claim symbolically, quite in line with his identity as a prophet who is cleansing the Temple. For them, Jesus refers to a spiritual or messianic renewal of the Temple and its function. Such a hope continued even after the destruction of the Herodian Temple and is echoed in the fourteenth of the Eighteen Benedictions recited in the synagogue. This benediction combines the expectation of a rebuilt Temple with the hope of a coming Messiah.

The evangelist's interpretation in verse 21, "he was speaking of the Temple of his body," is baffling from a Mediterranean cultural perspective which cherishes group orientation and commitment. Emphasis on the individual (body) is practically nonexistent because it would weaken and destroy a group.

The Qumran community viewed itself as the true temple of God's spirit. "Insofar as the laymen are concerned, [the community] will indeed be a temple [or sanctuary]; and insofar as the priesthood is concerned, it will indeed constitute the basis for a true 'holy of holies'" (see 1QS 8.7–10).

Paul, too, viewed the community as the temple in which the Spirit resides: "Or do you [Greek plural] not know that your [Greek plural, therefore collective] body is a temple [or sanctuary] of the Holy Spirit within you [Greek plural]?" (1 Cor 6:19).

That John identifies the risen body of Jesus (v. 21) rather than the community as the new Temple is culturally startling. From a purely Mediterranean cultural perspective, this individualistic interpretation could be the consequence of his group's distrust of all other groups (see Raymond Brown's *The Community of the Beloved Disciple*).

From a faith perspective, John says it all came clear after the resurrection (v. 22). How do culture and faith (understood as loyalty) relate to each other?

Fourth Sunday of Lent
John 3:14-21

One familiar sign waved by spectators at sports events in hopes that television cameras will transmit their message is: "John 3:16." A favorite of many Christians, this verse states: "God so loved the world that he gave his only Son, so that everyone who believes in him may not perish but have eternal life."

CONTEXT OF THE GOSPEL

Torn from its context (the entire Gospel of John and the Johannine community), this verse presents a heartwarming thought. The fuller literary context, as reported in today's reading, darkens the picture: "people loved darkness rather than light" (John 3:19).

For John, the term "world" carries a negative meaning. It includes both Judeans and Gentiles without distinction and describes those who refuse to accept or believe in Jesus. Opposition to the "world" is a dominant theme in John 14–17, yet the negative character of the "world" is evident throughout the Gospel.

The world is at odds with Jesus (16:20; 17:14, 16; 18:36) and with his Spirit (14:17; 16:8-11). Worse, it hates Jesus and those who believe in and follow after him (7:7; 15:18-19; 16:20). That the inhabitants of the world preferred darkness to light earns them the name "children of darkness" (12:35-36). For this reason, Jesus refuses to pray for the world; instead, he defeats the world (16:33).

Contemporary Christians, like those who wave the "John 3:16" signs at sporting events, ought to heed the caution of the eminent Johannine scholar, Raymond Brown, against the naiveté that this passage sometimes engenders. The world is not exclusively neutral, nor is it patiently awaiting good news. There are many who are actively hostile to Jesus, to Christianity and its message. Encountering the disbelief of the "world" was a shocking experience for the Johannine Christians. This knowledge should help their contemporary descendants to be forewarned and forearmed.

CONTEXT OF JOHN 3

Today's verses are selected from a more extensive discussion that Jesus had with Nicodemus, a Pharisee and "ruler" or "religious authority" among the Judeans of the house of Israel.

He was attracted to Jesus, but approaching him at night suggests that Nicodemus was trying to hide his interest (3:2). Anyone at all familiar with the nosey Mediterranean world where privacy is practically nonexistent can sympathize with Nicodemus' strategy to protect his reputation, his honor. Once ruined or lost, a reputation or honor cannot be regained.

But the discussion reported and interpreted by John runs in a circle because of Nicodemus' apparent failure to understand Jesus' use of a Greek word with two meanings: "again" and "from above" (3:3-9). Nicodemus typifies many who came to Jesus but had difficulty understanding him at first. Some never understood him (see John 2:23-25).

To his credit, though, Nicodemus seems to have pondered and perhaps even pursued his interest in Jesus further, no doubt in discussion with others in typically Mediterranean, group-centered fashion. Later in the Gospel (7:37-44), Jesus' statements in the Temple prompt a divided response in his audience. Some believe in him, and others want to arrest him.

The chief priests and Pharisees are disappointed and taunt and insult the Temple police for not arresting Jesus. At this moment, Nicodemus exposes himself to shame by defending Jesus' right to a hearing (vv. 50-51). Shame is not long in coming: "Surely you are not also from Galilee, are you?" ask his fellow Pharisees derisively. Nicodemus the night visitor has now gone one step further, to daytime defender of Jesus, at least indirectly.

The final appearance of Nicodemus in John's Gospel makes his spiritual journey appear to be complete. When Jesus dies, Nicodemus comes forward publicly with myrrh and aloes to anoint the body. He joins Joseph of Arimathea, a secret disciple of Jesus who feared the Judeans, and both of them see to the burial of Jesus' corpse (19:38-42).

This final appearance of Nicodemus illustrates John 3:14: "And just as Moses lifted up the serpent in the wilderness, so must the Son of Man be lifted up that whoever believes in him may have eternal life," and John 12:32: "And when I am lifted up from the earth, I will draw all people to myself." Lent is an opportune time to redirect one's path to Jesus.

Fifth Sunday of Lent
John 12:20-33

HONOR, THE FATHER, AND
SPIRITUAL PHENOMENA

Today's gospel selection resounds with themes of honor, the Middle Eastern core value that lies at the heart of understanding Jesus' passion, death, and resurrection. It helps bring chapter 12 and the Book of Signs to a conclusion.

Jesus declares that "the hour has come for the Son of Man to be glorified" (v. 23). He then prays: "Father, glorify your name!" and the Father responds: "I have glorified it and will glorify it again" (v. 28). The word "glorify" belongs to the semantic field of honor. It means "to assert or declare the honor" of the Son and the Father.

Throughout the first twelve chapters of this Gospel, Jesus has won arguments with opponents, worked seven signs, shared impressive and significant teaching with "his own people" (1:11), but they received him not. They denied his claims to honor.

Now Gentiles come to see Jesus and this appears to be the reason for his statement that at last he will receive the honorable recognition he deserves. The Greek word "to see" may also mean "to visit with" or "to meet." In John's heavily self-interpreted Gospel, however, the word probably has the meaning "to believe in"; there were still many who did not believe in Jesus despite the signs he worked.

Further, Jesus declares that the hour has come. Will he shirk it? Will he ask the Father to "save me from this hour?"

(v. 27). No, for it is precisely through his obedience unto death that he honors the Father's will, and the Father bestows honor by raising Jesus from the dead.

The parable of the seed (v. 24) indicates the means by which Jesus will be glorified. His death will be the source of life for many, actually for all (Israelites and non-Israelites). Moreover, those who follow Jesus will gain their entry to eternal life through death (vv. 25-26). For this reason, the one who is too attached to life in this world will not prove to be as honorable a follower of Jesus as the one who prefers life in the world to come. In eternity, the disciple will be with Jesus in the Father's love, an honorable status that nothing on earth can match.

The "voice from the sky" (v. 28) is yet another indication of Jesus' honorable reputation. In the Hebrew Scripture, this is the familiar *bat qol* or "daughter of the voice" of God which addressed the prophets. Some in the crowd think they have heard thunder (which was also considered the voice of God, see Ps 29); others think it the voice of an angel.

This event is yet another instance of Jesus momentarily experiencing alternate reality, that dimension of the real world inhabited by spiritual beings to which more than 90 percent of the world's cultures have routine and normal access (see the discussion of this point relative to the transfiguration of Jesus on the Second Sunday of Lent). Like the prophets, holy patriarchs, and others among his Mediterranean ancestors, Jesus regularly interacts with this reality.

The fact that the audience was not shocked or disturbed, but offered instead some of the commonly accepted explanations for this phenomenon, indicates that they were fully aware of Jesus' experience even though on this occasion no one else seemed to be participating in it with him. The "voice from heaven" is a culturally specific element in the Mediterranean alternate state of consciousness. All alternate states must be interpreted according to the traditional beliefs of their respective culture.

Newspaper and magazine reports that contemporary Westerners are hungering for more intimate contact with the spiritual world suggest an echo of the Gentile request of Andrew: "Sir, we would like to see [or believe in] Jesus."

Seeking a broker to establish contact with a patron is a common Mediterranean strategy.

Yet notice that Philip takes the request to Andrew, then both seem to lead the Greeks to Jesus. The group-centered Mediterranean world gives pause to Western individualists who might want to "do it alone, on my own, thank you very much." Lenten communal observances in many churches, such as educational programs or devotional activities, provide a golden opportunity "to see, visit with, and come to a deeper faith in Jesus."

Passion Sunday
Mark 14:1–15:47

In Mark's passion story, of the Twelve disciples hand picked by Jesus one betrayed him (14:10), another denied him (14:66-72), and all abandoned him at his greatest moment of need (14:50). If these intimate followers of Jesus were absent for all the events of the passion, where did Mark obtain the information he reports?

Some scholars believe that the story already existed in a relatively fixed form prior to any evangelist's writing. Mark simply reported what tradition had already formulated. Others believe that Mark crafted the story of Jesus' passion and death as an integral part of his Gospel. Still others, noting many allusions to the Hebrew Scriptures such as Psalms 22 and 69 and the Servant Songs of Isaiah, propose that the story took shape in liturgical commemorations of Jesus' death. As the early followers of Jesus reflected upon his suffering and death, they resorted to the Hebrew Bible for insight. This was the only Scripture they knew. Very likely a combination of all these elements contributed to the composition of Mark's passion story.

While traditional Scripture scholarship on the passion narrative focuses on the relationship of tradition to the creative activity of the evangelist, some contemporary scholars look to Mediterranean culture for brighter light. Culture offers at least two insights: honor and shame, and pain and suffering.

HONOR AND SHAME

The Mediterranean core values of honor and shame resonate throughout. During Jesus' lifetime, no antagonist succeeded in shaming him. Jesus successfully protected his honor against all attacks. By contrast in the passion, a tradition older than the rest of the Gospel narratives, Jesus seems to be shamed by both his intimate followers and his enemies. It is difficult to understand why this master of riposte in the rest of the Gospel remains mute in the passion story.

On the one hand, he wins eminent Mediterranean cultural honor by dying with a degree of manliness (machismo) which impresses the pagan centurion (15:39). On the other hand, there is no denying that crucifixion was a shameful punishment reserved for criminals such as those at Jesus' left and right (15:27).

Our Mediterranean ancestors in the faith who understood honor and shame perfectly perceived these conflicting aspects of the story quite clearly. But a closer reading of the story demonstrates how the Mediterranean shapers of this passion tradition intended to show that Jesus turned the shameful experience into something very honorable. The woman who anoints Jesus (14:3-9) anticipates the honor that has to be omitted at his burial (15:46). In his agony, the dutiful son honorably pledges to do the will of his Father no matter how repulsive (14:36).

At the inquisition by the chief priests and the Sanhedrin, the "false" charge (14:58-64) of Jesus' messianic identity is an ironic statement of his true honorable status. In his meeting with Pilate the procurator, Jesus "the King" holds a higher status and therefore behaves with cultural correctness in ignoring Pilate, an inferior (15.2-5). Those who mock him also honor him ironically (15:16-20). And the fact that God raises Jesus from the dead confirms this honor in a way no human accolade ever could (16:1-8). Mediterranean readers see in the passion story an ironic pronouncement of Jesus' true honor.

PAIN AND SUFFERING

Unimpressed with honor and shame, Western readers tend to focus on Jesus' intense physical suffering: scourging, crowning with thorns, crucifixion. In Western culture, pain and suffering are experienced by the body and therefore should be avoided and eliminated. Why didn't Jesus avoid it? What did he hope to gain by suffering?

In contrast, Jesus and his culture shared the beliefs common to the entire ancient world since the time of Aristotle. The soul, not the body, feels pain and suffering, and therefore they can never be eliminated but only alleviated. Stoic, Pythagorean, Jesus', and all ancient responses to pain are based on that belief. By bearing his excruciating suffering in Mediterranean manly fashion Jesus demonstrated filial obedience to his Father.

It is fashionable today in the United States to respect and celebrate cultural diversity. The passion story of Jesus provides an opportunity for modern Western believers to do just that.

Easter Sunday
John 20:1-9

One can only admire the cleverness of the architects of the Lectionary who assigned this same gospel reading for Easter Sunday morning in all three cycles of the liturgical year. The evangelist reports the reactions of Mary Magdalene ("the body was stolen," v. 2), John ("he saw and believed," v. 8), and Peter (he observed everything, said nothing, and went home with the others, vv. 6-7, 10).

FAITH

Commentators have long puzzled over the evangelist's parenthetical comment: "Remember that as yet they did not understand the Scripture that Jesus had to rise from the dead" (v. 9). What could this mean if John "saw and believed"? Perhaps "they" should refer only to Mary Magdalene and Peter?

Students of the Gospels know that they contain at least three layers of tradition, and John's Gospel sometimes contains more. There is no doubt that this story reflects the evangelist's conflation of a number of traditions, which is responsible for some of the difficulty in understanding it. This development is traced in many traditional studies such as Raymond Brown's Anchor Bible *Commentary on the Gospel of John*.

In these present reflections, we turn for fresh insight to a new book, *Biblical Social Values and their Meaning* (Hendrickson Publishers, 1993), in which biblical scholar Bruce Malina explains that in the ancient Mediterranean world "faith" primarily describes loyalty and commitment to another person. A faithful person is a reliable person, one who manifests enduring personal loyalty or personal faithfulness "no matter what." In other words, faith can be viewed as a social glue that binds people together in this world.

It seems clear that this is the meaning John the evangelist intends too. His community was deeply concerned about loyalty, solidarity, and cohesiveness in the face of a hostile world. The need for such enduring loyalty to Jesus is evident in the frequency with which the evangelist uses the words "faith" and "to believe." Indeed, he uses a wide array of synonyms to make the same point: "to come to," "to abide in," "to follow after," "to love," "to keep the words of," "to receive," "to have," "to see."

Thus, the Beloved Disciple who came to the empty tomb and "saw and believed" had a different response to the experience than did Mary Magdalene (who suspected theft) and Peter (who apparently didn't conclude anything). John saw troubling things (an empty tomb, no corpse, abandoned wrappings), but remained "loyal, no matter what" (= believed). If one accepts this cultural interpretation, the parenthetical remark about not yet understanding the Scripture can apply even to the disciple who believed.

American "believers" will find this explanation very challenging. In American culture, faith bears a strong intellectual character. It looks primarily to the mind rather than to the heart and will.

Because American culture in particular and Western culture in general is so rational, the word "faith" takes on the further nuance of requiring a word of authority, particularly when the evidence is lacking or weak. The fact that there is no heavenly messenger or anyone else in today's scene to deliver such an authoritative word makes the Beloved Disciple's normal Mediterranean response very puzzling to an American reader.

This rational (and non-Mediterranean) dimension of faith is so central in American medicine, for instance, that a placebo is invariably effective: the person receiving it believes that the person administering it (even if an impostor or an actor) is an authority who is qualified and deserving of trust.

The contrast between the Mediterranean understanding of faith and that of the modern Western believer is particularly challenging on Easter Sunday, the central feast of the Christian calendar. The Beloved Disciple sees troubling evidence but remains committed to Jesus "no matter what." In contrast, Americans speak of "rats jumping off a sinking ship," describing a common experience of opportunist friends and allies who abandon a wounded or weakened friend in difficult times. Today's gospel provides a splendid opportunity for American believers to reconsider their occasionally excessively rational approach to life and the impediment that might pose to "real faith" or loyalty.

Second Sunday of Easter
John 20:19-31

The various gospel accounts of Jesus' resurrection appearances reflect a variety of traditions that are not easy to reconcile. Today's reading is set "on the evening of that first day of the week," but the "disciples" (v. 19; are there more than Eleven?) gathered together seem unaware of Peter's, John's, and Mary Magdalene's experiences at the empty tomb "early" on that same day (as recounted in vv. 1-10).

Scholars recognize that the evangelists received a diversity of traditions which they proceeded to interpret still further according to the "situation of the churches" for which they wrote and the particular purpose each author set for himself (*Pontifical Biblical Commission Instruction on the Historical Truth of the Gospels,* 1964, no. 9). John the evangelist reported the tradition of frightened disciples gathered behind locked doors and added to it a story he created about "doubting Thomas" (vv. 24-29; see the reflection on this passage in cycle C for details). This new composition formed a larger scene to explain how the risen Jesus commissioned the disciples to bring new members into the community (vv. 19-21; see the reflection on this theme in cycle A).

Why do the resurrection appearances receive such diverse interpretations in the Gospels? To answer this question, we need to understand the pan-human experience known as altered states of consciousness and the distinctive function or role this experience plays in individual cultures.

APPEARANCES AND MEDITERRANEAN CULTURE

Ninety percent of the world's cultures normally and routinely experience altered states of consciousness; that is, they get a glimpse of an alternate reality that is richer than the reality they experience most often. Eighty percent of the Mediterranean societies investigated by researchers, including the Hebrews, Greeks, and ancient Egyptians, have had these same experiences. Physician-anthropologists observe that Western societies in general, and the United States in particular, appear to have successfully blocked out this normal human capability (see the comments on the transfiguration of Jesus, Second Sunday of Lent above).

Still, even in these societies, dreams are one familiar and common experience of alternate reality. Dreams are not bounded by time. From the dreamer's perspective, the dead consort with the living, and experiences separated by clock and calendar in waking consciousness flow together. Bible readers know that dreams are commonly reported in Scripture (e.g., Gen 37:5-11; Matt 1:20-24; 2:12; 2:13 14; etc.).

Visions are another experience of alternate reality reported frequently in the Bible (Num 12:6; 1 Sam 3:16; Ezek 8:3; 40:1-2; Matt 17:9; etc.). It is culturally plausible to include appearances of the risen Jesus in the category of experiences of alternate reality, or states of altered consciousness.

FUNCTION OF RESURRECTION APPEARANCES

Church guidelines remind Bible readers of the necessity to distinguish various layers or stages of tradition in interpreting the Gospels. At rock bottom lies the tradition of the events of the life of Jesus, the apostles and all who interacted with them. The second stage of tradition is what the apostles preached about what they remembered of Jesus' words and deeds. And the third stage is that of the evangelist writing between forty to sixty years after Jesus' lifetime on earth.

Since the experience of alternate reality is normal and common in Mediterranean societies, it is possible that those who saw the risen Jesus experienced him in an altered state of consciousness. They caught a glimpse of risen life, a reality that truly exists and includes much more than does ordinary human consciousness.

The function of such experiences in the Mediterranean world is to guide people through otherwise insoluble difficulties and problems. When in doubt about a course of action, or the proper solution to a problem, Mediterranean people seek help and enlightenment in alternate reality. They know how to enter and exit this dimension of human experience as easily as Westerners know how to drive a car, program VCRs, and enjoy their CDs.

At the second and third levels of tradition reflected in the Scriptures, the preachers and evangelists sometimes reported the tradition they received (the appearances of the risen Jesus) and at other times created a tradition that would reflect common, Mediterranean cultural experience (the doubting Thomas story).

While modern science has blessed Western believers many times over, today's gospel highlights one area of human experience it may have impoverished. Efforts to regain this gift of God could pay rich spiritual dividends.

Third Sunday of Easter
Luke 24:35-48

This appearance of the risen Jesus to the Christian community follows the story of his appearances to the two disciples at Emmaus. The complete unit (vv. 36-53) can be divided into three scenes: (1) the appearance (vv. 36-43); (2) instruction and a final commission (vv. 44-49); (3) the ascension (vv. 50-53).

THE APPEARANCE

If we explore this appearance story in terms of alternate reality, some of its elements make fresh sense. First, the disciples exhibit multiple reactions: they are terrified and startled (v. 37), alarmed and skeptical (v. 38), overjoyed yet wondering (v. 40), and they think they see a "ghost" (Greek: "spirit," v. 34), which suggests that they recognize a new kind of experience.

They know Jesus died and was buried, but now they see him quite alive. Instead of a "ghost" they see a flesh and bone person in alternate reality (v. 39). Jesus eats fish in their presence (v. 43) not only to prove his "reality" but to reestablish table fellowship with his followers! Clearly this is a new kind of experience of alternate reality.

NEW UNDERSTANDING

As the disciples at Emmaus so too does this community gain a new understanding of the risen Jesus they are experiencing, rooted in the Scripture. Jesus personally "opened their minds" to the fuller meaning of the words he spoke in his lifetime

73

and offered a deeper understanding of the Hebrew Scriptures. No specific passages from the Old Testament are cited. Indeed, scholars are unable to find any passages that relate to Luke's global interpretation that "the Messiah shall suffer and rise from the dead on the third day."

In the Torah, the word "Messiah" refers only to the anointed high priest (see Lev 4:3, 5, 16; 6:15) and never to an expected Davidic king who is to suffer. In the Prophets, the title "Messiah" refers to a historical king that would sit on David's throne (1 Sam 24:7; 2 Sam 2:10, 38; etc.). Second Isaiah (45:1) ascribed the title to Cyrus of Persia! Only in Daniel 9:25 does one meet for the first time in the Old Testament a reference to "an anointed one, a prince" as Messiah. In the Psalms it refers mainly to David (2:2; 132:10, 17). No matter. The Father's will has been fulfilled, and only in the light of the resurrection can Scripture be fully understood.

Experiences of alternate reality opened the minds of prophets and others in the Old Testament to understanding the will of God with greater clarity and precision; the experience of the risen Jesus accomplishes the same result for those who see him.

COMMISSION

What then is the function of this specific experience of alternate reality? In today's passage, the risen Jesus commissions "the Eleven and their companions" (Luke 24:33) to preach "repentance for the forgiveness of sins" to all nations and to be "witnesses" (vv. 47-48).

Preaching forgiveness of sins is a familiar theme in Luke, but the theme of testimony is a new one that will be highlighted repeatedly throughout Acts. These eyewitness followers now bear witness and testimony to the end of the earth concerning the suffering Messiah who was raised (e.g., Acts 4:4, 29, 31, etc.).

EMPOWERMENT

Ordinarily, the experience of alternate reality itself suffices to convince, motivate, and empower the recipient to act upon the experience. But Jesus advises his followers to "remain here in the city until you are invested with power from on high" (v. 49).

This is a crucial notion in Luke's Gospel, unfortunately omitted in the selection assigned for today's liturgy. It was with the "power of the Lord" that Jesus healed people (Luke 5:17). Indeed, the "power that went forth from him" (Luke 6:19) is the very same power with which God will invest these disciples (Luke 24:49; Acts 1:5).

The fact that it is impossible to harmonize the diverse resurrection stories into a continuous narrative should give the modern believer pause. One transforming experience of the risen Jesus and its narration in a single story sufficed for our ancestors in the faith. The experience and/or the story was enlightening and empowering.

Through centuries of Christian tradition, this experience has been stylized in ritual and relived in sacrament. The Western tendency toward rationalization has often robbed liturgy, ritual, and sacrament of their potential experiential impact. Can today's reflections help restore the power?

Fourth Sunday of Easter
John 10:11-18

Nothing in John's Gospel is as simple as it seems. Today's topic, the noble shepherd, began in cycle A (10:1-10) and will conclude in cycle C (10:27-30). Central to these passages is the Mediterranean understanding of sheep and shepherds.

In today's selection, the Johannine Jesus points to himself as the noble shepherd who contrasts starkly with the hireling. Five times Jesus the noble shepherd refers to "laying down his life" for the sheep while the hireling is frightened by the mere sight of the approaching wolf and flees, leaving the sheep to the predator.

Jerome Neyrey enlarges the picture for us. His Johannine research demonstrates how John the evangelist casts Jesus as the noble shepherd (e.g., he feeds his sheep, 13:26). The Beloved Disciple is also a noble shepherd, but Peter the braggart is portrayed as the hireling who abandons the sheep to the wolf. He has miles to go before he can be elevated to the rank of shepherd.

THE BELOVED DISCIPLE

From the very first moment that he appears in the Gospel, the Beloved Disciple is clearly special. He is "the one whom Jesus loved" (13:23), who is an intimate friend of Jesus (reclining at his side, 13:23), and who obtains for Peter inside information from Jesus (13:24-26). The modern reader is stunned to see Peter dependent upon this disciple for access to Jesus!

As the story progresses, the Beloved Disciple follows Jesus closely through his moments of crises to Caiaphas' house and even to the cross. This disciple risks his very life by being so closely associated with Jesus. Peter, it is true, cut off the ear of Malchus the high priest's servant while trying to defend Jesus in the garden, but Jesus ordered him to put away his sword (John 19:10-11). Peter did the wrong thing.

The noble shepherd enters by the door (10:2). The Beloved Disciple, known to the high priest, entered into his house but Peter stood outside (18:15). The noble shepherd commands the gatekeeper to open the door (10:2-3); the Beloved Disciple, known to the high priest, requests the maid who kept the door to open it (10:16). The noble shepherd calls the sheep by name and leads them (10:3-4); at the request of the Beloved Disciple, the maid led Peter in (18:16). At this point in the story, the Beloved Disciple is clearly a shepherd, Peter is only a sheep.

PETER

At the Last Supper, Jesus washes the feet of the disciples including Peter (John 13:6-11). Neyrey identifies this as a ritual that is a nonrepeatable strategy for crossing a boundary, for transforming status. Baptism is ritual, a nonrepeatable strategy that transforms a nonbeliever into a believer and carries the candidates across the boundary into the community of believers.

Peter has already proved his loyalty to Jesus (6:67-69) and is already a member of the general circle of disciples (see 9:28). In John 13:8, Jesus offers Peter the insider a "part" or "inheritance" with him. This is a new "clean" status, a more perfect role (in contrast to Judas who is "not clean" 13:2, 11). But Peter does not fully understand what Jesus is doing (13:7, 9-10).

Peter's misunderstanding is more fully played out a few verses later when he insists that he will lay down his life for Jesus (13:37; compare 10:11), and Jesus predicts that Peter will rather deny him three times (13:38). Peter will be a disloyal coward (18:17, 25-27), behaving like a hireling, before his final, post-resurrection transformation into noble shepherd (21:15, 16, 17). Only then does Peter repair his lapsed loyalty with a threefold declaration of love. Indeed, after the

Resurrection Jesus predicts Peter's death (21:18-19) acknowledging that Peter's earlier pledge (13:38) will ultimately find fulfillment.

Nothing in John's Gospel is as simple as it seems. This small reflection on the noble shepherd binds together for contrast some key figures: Jesus, Peter, Judas, and the Beloved Disciple. In the Johannine community, where the Beloved Disciple was highly esteemed, it must have been difficult to demonstrate that Peter and not the Beloved Disciple was the shepherd of the group.

Peter's transformation from disloyal coward to noble shepherd offers much food for thought to Americans who seem driven to put their leaders—secular and religious— through intense moral scrutiny. Peter would be the last person to throw stones.

Fifth Sunday of Easter
John 15:1-8

In the Mediterranean world, even God needs honor! "My Father has been honored [= glorified] in this," says Jesus, "in your bearing much fruit and becoming my disciples" (John 15:8). The social reality that stands behind this statement is the Mediterranean institution of patronage.

PATRONAGE

In societies where central government is weak and ineffective, people have to look after their own needs. Most often they help each other by bartering or trading. When social equals are unable to help each other, they must seek someone with greater means who is expected to play the role of patron.

A patron freely chooses clients and serves them by giving them goods they are unable to obtain by their own efforts or on terms better than they could obtain. The people of Israel viewed and behaved toward their God as their patron. The people considered themselves clients, and key people like prophets were considered brokers. In the New Testament world, Jesus clearly presents himself as a broker of God the patron who heals, sends rain, and bestows other favors upon his clients.

VINE IMAGERY

The imagery of "remaining in" Jesus the "true" vine (vv. 4-7) which has replaced the former vine, Israel (see Isa 5:1-7), reflects the normal and expected Middle Eastern "solidarity"

79

between client and patron, even to the point of the client's self-effacement. The client's bond with the patron must be single-minded and single-hearted. Life itself depends upon it.

BEARING FRUIT

On a vine, every living branch is expected to bear fruit. If a branch does not bear fruit, it is considered to be dead despite other signs of life and is pruned away (v. 2). It is too simplistic to interpret "bearing fruit" as a reference to performing good works and leading an exemplary life. The responsible vine dresser will not allow a non-fruit-bearing branch to sap precious life from the vine.

God the patron is honored when clients draw their life from Jesus the vine who is also the patron's broker. Sustaining life is one of the patron's major gifts to the client. The client must accept and embrace the gift of life and "bear fruit." The meaning of this phrase will become clear shortly.

BECOMING DISCIPLES

A client can never repay the munificence of a patron. Instead, a grateful client publicizes the patron's generosity far and wide. This is how the patron's honor is proclaimed, maintained, and even augmented.

The broker shares in this honor, too, because the broker benefits every time the patron benefits and vice-versa. If God the patron's clients become disciples of Jesus his broker, God the patron benefits in double measure. The number of those who proclaim God's honor continues to grow.

Now we can begin to understand the meaning of "bearing fruit." Jesus proposes that ultimately this tri-personal (patron-broker-client) symbiotic relationship should blossom into friendship (v. 15) characterized by love demonstrated in the willingness to lay down one's life for one's friends. Jesus himself is the model of such loving friendship.

But the evangelist is writing these words to Christians living in the last decade of the first century, under Roman domination, and threatened by political harassment and persecution. He wishes to encourage and strengthen fearful believers. He recalls Jesus' words "if they persecuted me, they will persecute you" (15:20) and his advice that "apart from me you can do nothing" (15:5). Readers will also remember Jesus' earlier comment: "if [a grain of wheat falls to the ground and dies], it produces much fruit" (John 12:24).

How does one honor God by bearing much fruit? Pilate consented to Jesus' execution when Jesus' enemies warned that any other decision would indicate that "you are not Caesar's friend" (John 19:12). In the vine passage, John reminds his readers that it is more important to remain Jesus' friend, and through that God's friend, than to preserve one's life.

What can American believers learn from the Mediterranean style of solidarity (vine and branches) lived by their ancestors in the faith?

Sixth Sunday of Easter
John 15:9-17

John's Gospel is permeated with the word "love." In today's eight verses the word occurs eight times! Of particular interest is Jesus' advice that his followers "love one another" (vv. 12, 17) "as I love you" (v. 12). How did our Mediterranean ancestors in the faith understand this word?

LOVE = ATTACHMENT

In the Mediterranean world, affection is not central to the concept of love. It may be present, but more often than not it isn't. The key element in the Mediterranean understanding of love is attachment and bonding, particularly to the group. Joshua exhorts the people "to love the Lord your God . . . and to hold fast to him" (Josh 22:5). "Solomon clung to these [his foreign wives] in love" (1 Kgs 11:2).

The familiar quotation "therefore a man leaves his father and his mother and clings to his wife, and they become one flesh" (Gen 2:23) is particularly enlightening in understanding group attachment. According to Middle Eastern custom, a married son continues to live with his father and mother in his father's house. "Leaving" father and mother therefore means dis-attaching himself from them in order to attach himself to his wife. While he "cleaves" to his wife, however, his primary group attachment is still to his father and brothers and the household.

John develops the theme of attachment (= love) throughout his Gospel. For instance, God was so attached to humanity that he sent his only Son (3:16) to whom also God is very attached (17:24-26). In the series of challenges and ripostes exchanged between Jesus and the Pharisees Jesus questions their claim that God is their Father: "If God were your Father, you would love me for I came from God." Rephrased, Jesus' objection is that if his opponents were attached to him who came from God it would be clear that they are indeed attached to the Father. But since they are not attached to Jesus, they cannot be attached to the Father. Throughout John's Gospel, Jesus repeatedly invites and exhorts his disciples to be attached to him (14:15, 21, 23, 24; 21:15-17).

LOVE INVOLVES DOING

Generally speaking, "being" is the primary preference in the Middle Eastern value system. This means that Middle Easterners generally opt for spontaneous response to the stimulus of the moment, like children in the market place who should respond immediately to cues to dance or mourn (Matt 11:16-17). People who don't respond appropriately are considered uncooperative, which definitely does not promote and solidify group attachment.

In this same value system, "doing," that is, calculated and planned activity, is a secondary option. In today's passage, Jesus urges the disciples to "keep [– do] my commandments" (v. 10) and "do what I command you" (v. 14). A survey of any of the Gospels reveals that he repeats this exhortation rather frequently. Why is this necessary?

In most cultures, the primary value orientation represents male choices. For females in the culture, the options are reversed. For males in the Mediterranean world, the values that regulate activity are "being," then "doing." For females, the order is "doing," then "being."

In his ministry, Jesus sought to invert the order of these values according to the needs of the moment. Martha who was quite appropriately "doing" (primary orientation for Mediterranean women) was directed to imitate Mary's "being" (spontaneous response to Jesus at the moment, Luke 10:38-42).

Here in John 15 addressing his (presumably) male disciples, Jesus says "being" (love-attachment to him and the

Father) is not enough. They must strive to "do" (keep the commandments; do what I command you).

Throughout the Hebrew Bible, the prophets had to prod Israel to similar behavior. The nation believed that simply "being chosen" by God sufficed. This conferred honorable status. What else was needed? Each prophet challenged the people to "keep" the covenant, to "obey" the commandments, to "perform deeds of justice and charity," because this was not the normal cultural script.

The preference for goal-setting and planned activity in Western culture and the corresponding difficulty in "hanging loose" therefore sounds like it is just what the prophets and Jesus were after. If they had to preach to Americans today, what would the message be?

Seventh Sunday of Easter
John 17:11-19

On the Fourth Sunday of Lent in this cycle, we reflected on John's presentation of the "world" as the forces that are hostile to Jesus and his followers. Today's reading is another example of that sentiment.

How did Jesus cope with this hostility? How does he expect his disciples to cope with it? The Johannine Jesus prays (17:1-26) first for his immediate disciples (vv. 6-19) and then for all who will later come to believe in him (vv. 20-26).

PRAYER

From a purely cultural perspective, prayer is an act of communication intended to have an impact on a person perceived as being in control of life in order to obtain results from that person. Not all prayer is religious prayer. Mary's comment to Jesus at the wedding that "they have no wine" is a nonreligious prayer, an act of communication intended to influence Jesus to act on the couple's behalf (John 2:3). The prayer of Jesus in today's passage is a religious prayer because it is addressed to God: "Jesus looked up to heaven and said, 'Father, the hour has come'" (John 17:1).

Two key features of religious prayer are (1) that it is communication to God (2) intended to obtain specific results.

COMMUNICATION TO GOD

Jesus addresses God as "Holy Father" (v. 11), and the tone of the prayer reveals the attachment or solidarity between

Father and Son as well as Jesus' firm commitment to fulfilling the will of his Father.

DESIRED RESULTS

Jesus asks the Father to protect his disciples in the world (v. 11) and from the "evil one" (v. 15), and to sanctify them in the truth (v. 17).

Protection

In Jesus' group-centered culture, no individual ever feels capable of taking on the "world" singlehandedly. In his moment of crisis, Jesus reminds the belligerent Peter to put his sword back into its sheath: "Do you think that I cannot appeal to my Father, and he will at once send me more than twelve legions of angels?" (Matt 26:53).

As difficulties in the Mediterranean world affect groups and not just individuals, so protection must come from a group and not just an individual. The group known as "the world" is opposed to the group comprised of Jesus and his disciples. Engagements between these groups have been very difficult, and the Jesus group suffered one loss (v. 12) because the evil one is on the "other" side (see John 6:70; 13:2, 27). The only way to get an edge on such a powerful enemy is to petition the help of an even more powerful ally, the heavenly Father (vv. 11, 15).

Sanctification

The Old Testament tradition urged that God's people sanctify themselves: "be holy, for I am holy" (Lev 11:44; 19:2; 20:26). Holiness and sanctification involve separation from what is not holy. Because the disciples belong to God (v. 9) they must separate themselves from the forces that are opposed to God (the world).

Moreover, the disciples are to be sanctified in the truth which is God's word (v. 19). But since Jesus is both Word and truth (John 14:6), the disciples are to be separate from the world so that they can be more strongly attached to Jesus. Indeed, they have accepted the word Jesus brought them (v. 14) and are thus prepared for mission (v. 18), that is, the disciples are now able to share the word with others.

It is difficult not to conclude that Jesus' prayer for his disciples reflects something of a siege mentality: "us" against "them." There was certainly good reason for this feeling in Jesus' lifetime, and equally good reason for it when the evangelist was writing, some sixty years after Jesus died.

The contemporary Christian who would like to draw inspiration or guidance for life from a passage like this must strive to balance the need for separateness with the advantage of being open and available to all, even one's enemies. Prayer understood in the cultural perspective can be of some help.

Religious prayer is primarily communication to God but the public prayers we hear often seem crafted (primarily?) to impress the listeners! Jesus' prayer in this passage is addressed to the Father but delivered within earshot of his disciples! How many purposes does prayer serve in the life of your community?

Pentecost
John 20:19-23

Each year this same Scripture passage is read on Pentecost. In the volume on cycle A, we reflect on the Spirit, and in the volume on cycle C we reflect on the commissioning of the disciples. Here we reflect upon the themes of fear and joy.

FEAR

Contemporary psychiatric research notes that anxiety and fear are related emotions, and both relate to action. Fear stimulates avoidance and escape, but when these or any actions are blocked or thwarted, fear turns into anxiety. At the core, all emotions presuppose certain kinds of knowledge. In fear, this knowledge is an awareness of danger.

Johannine scholar Raymond Brown points out that in the Synoptic Gospels, the guards and women are frightened by the sight of the angel at the tomb (Mark 16:8; Matt 28:4, 5, 8; Luke 24:5), and the women and disciples are frightened by the sight of Jesus (Matt 28:10; Luke 24:37). Though Middle Easterners readily interact with the world of the spirits, these contacts always stir fear because of their potential danger. One is never certain of the nature of the spirit (good, bad, mischievous) or of the possible outcome of the encounter.

In John's Gospel, it is not encounters with spirits but rather "the Judeans" who cause fear (see also John 7:13). At the time of Jesus, there could be any number of reasons why the disciples would fear the Judeans. They had belonged to Jesus' faction and hence could expect to experience the same persecution as he did from Judean authorities. After Jesus' resurrection, they might be sought by these same authorities for alleged complicity in stealing the corpse (Matt 28:13) and spreading a lie. A third source of fear is reported in the Gospel of Peter (26): a widespread search for the disciples was instituted on the grounds that they were malefactors and had attempted to burn the Temple.

Fear on these or any similar grounds would certainly account for the highly irregular action of "locking the doors." Middle Eastern culture does not recognize or respect privacy. While the interior of a house is sacred to the family, the place where the women are protected and kept secure, children have the culturally recognized right of wandering in and out of every home to spy on what other families are doing and report this back to their own families.

In group-oriented societies like that of our ancestors in the faith, every group suspects that all other groups are plotting evil against it. The only way to protect one's group is to keep informed about what other groups are up to. Young children serve this purpose, which is why Jesus forbade his disciples to keep the youngsters away from him. Jesus wanted everyone to know that he had nothing to hide.

The reason why the disciples locked the door is chiefly because they wanted to hide themselves! Not that others did not know where they were or could not easily find them. Their action (locking doors = avoidance) was prompted by fear.

PEACE

Typically in the Bible, when a supernatural being encounters a human being, the supernatural being assures the human of its good will. Words like "do not be afraid" (Luke 1:13, 30; 2:10; Matt 28:5, 10; etc.) set the human being at ease and dispel the fear.

The Hebrew word for "peace" is very rich and has at least eight different meanings. David asks his general, Joab, literally about "the peace of Joab, the peace of the people, and the peace of the war" (2 Sam 11:7). When Jesus says to his frightened disciples, "Peace to you," he declares a factual reality. His resurrection has gained unshakable peace for them;

hence it is inappropriate to translate his statement as a wish: "[May] peace be to [or with] you." Jesus is not wishing them peace; he declares with firm assurance that they possess it, hence they should discard all fear.

And indeed they do. Their new knowledge immediately replaces the old perceptions that stirred fear and anxiety. As the risen Lord commissions them to receive new members into the community, they recognize a new beginning and not an end for those who believe in him.

Trinity
Matthew 28:16-20

Increasingly, scholarly biblical research makes headlines. In recent years, articles in *Time, Newsweek, U.S. News and World Report, The Wall Street Journal,* and other purely secular periodicals have given more publicity to scholarly conclusions than these scholars might ever have dreamed of from the technical journals and books in which their conclusions first appeared. Yet very often, the conclusions have been known and accepted for a long time in the scholarly community before they became known to the wider public.

What do scholars say about today's reading from Matthew's Gospel? As Bishop Descamps noted long ago, as far as substance goes, the Gospels present various versions of the same appearance to the Twelve. Each Gospel singles out an all-important appearance of Jesus to the disciples in which they are commissioned for a task.

JESUS' EDICT

Today's scene is found only in Matthew, and careful study of the vocabulary and style indicates that Matthew creatively composed this passage. The language echoes that of Daniel 7:14 (Septuagint), but other influences may well have been Exodus 19–20, the familiar blessing in Numbers 6:22-27, various prophetic commissions, and the royal decree of Cyrus in 2 Chronicles 36:23.

Just as an "edict" of Cyrus concludes 2 Chronicles, the last book in the Hebrew Bible, so does an "edict" by the risen

Jesus conclude the Book of Matthew. Cyrus, the Persian king, proclaimed: "The Lord, the God of heaven, has given me all the kingdoms of the earth, and has charged me to build him a house at Jerusalem, which is in Judah. Whoever is among you of all his people, may the Lord his God be with him! Let him go up."

Jesus' edict has three parts: a command (v. 16: go to the mountain), a response (v. 17: when the apostles saw him, some worshipped but some doubted), and another command (vv. 18-20: make disciples of all the Gentiles; baptize and teach them).

Jesus' edict is a startling challenge to Matthew's community. Earlier during his ministry, Jesus sent the disciples on mission only to the Judeans: "Go nowhere among the Gentiles, enter no town of the Samaritans, but go rather to the lost sheep of the house of Israel" (Matt 10:5-6).

This attitude is typical of group-centered societies. They tend to be exclusivistic and divide the world into two camps: them and us, the good and those who aren't. Cultural specialists readily admit that this often spills over into a prejudice, that is, a negative evaluation, based on race (biology) or ethnicity (behavior), and rooted in an organized predisposition toward negative evaluations.

As Matthew has composed it in 80–85 C.E., the message of the risen Lord challenges a largely Judean-Christian group to seek new members from among non-Judeans. Yet this should not have been entirely unexpected. There were hints in this direction throughout the Gospel (2:1-12; 4:15, 16, 23-25; 8:5-13; 10:18; 15:21-28; 22:1-10; 24:14; 24:32; 26:13).

Perhaps the community had already attracted as many Judeans as it could hope to in Matthew's time, and thus there was a need to open a new mission field. Clearly, a major separation between Church and synagogue is well on its way.

As a summary of Matthew's Gospel, today's passage highlights key themes: It is the Father who has given Jesus ultimate and universal authority. Jesus in turn directs his followers to move beyond their in-group to the entire world, particularly to those who do not share the same ethnic roots. Difficult as this may be, Jesus assures his followers of his abiding presence until the reign of God is established in all its fullness.

TRINITY

Biblical scholars agree that the theological notion of the Trinity is a later development with roots in Scripture. Theologians trace the development through the various disputes in the first thousand years of the Church's existence. Liturgists credit Benedictine monasteries of the ninth and eleventh centuries with being instrumental in promoting liturgical prominence for the Trinity. The Franciscan Pope John XXII decreed that the Divine Office of the Blessed Trinity should be observed by the entire Church (1334).

A sense of history is a valuable tool for appreciating the origin and development of basic Christian beliefs.

Corpus Christi
Mark 14:12-16, 22-26

Reading this familiar passage from a first-century, Middle Eastern cultural perspective adds fresh insight to a cherished event in Jesus' life.

PASSOVER CEREMONY

Scholars agree that John's report is historically more probable than the Synoptic report. The meal Jesus shared with his disciples was not a Passover meal (see John 13:1-2). Jesus was crucified just as Passover was beginning (John 18:28; 19:31). Mark and the other Synoptics have given the meal a Passover interpretation in part because they wanted to demonstrate that Jesus faithfully observed traditional customs.

Notice also, quite in accord with the culture, that the meal was prepared by the males. "You shall observe this rite as an ordinance for you and your sons for ever" (Exod 12:3, 4, 24). Women prepared ordinary meals. One, usually a widow, served the men who ate first together with the boys past the age of puberty. Women, girls, and boys under the age of puberty ate separately and later.

In Jerusalem, Jesus had a disciple upon whom he could rely to provide a place for himself and the Twelve to celebrate this ceremony. A man carrying a water jar would be very easy to spot. Drawing and carrying water was a woman's task (Gen 24:11), and any man present at the well or spring would be a challenge to the honor of all the fathers, brothers, and husbands with whom the women gathered were associated.

If a man did carry water, it was more often in a skin than a jar. Women carry water in a jar balanced upon their heads. Men carry it in a skin slung over the shoulder or under the arm. A man carrying a water jar (Mark 14:13) is a cultural anomaly, easy to spot.

COMMON MEAL

Anthropologists identify meals in antiquity as ceremonies rather than rituals. A ritual (like baptism) effects a change in status, but a ceremony is a regular and predictable occurrence which confirms and legitimates people's roles and status in a community.

Eating together implies that people also share common ideas and values, and often common social status as well (see Mark 2:15-17 for the implications of Jesus' choice of meal partners). People in antiquity paid close attention to who ate with whom, who sat where (Luke 14:7-11), what people ate and drank (Luke 7:33-34) and where (Mark 6:35-36), how the food was prepared (John 21:9), which utensils were used (Mark 7:4), when the meal took place (Passover, Mark 14:12; before Passover, John 13:1-2), what was discussed at table (Luke 22:24-39, part of which was reported on the way to the garden in Matt 26.30-35 and Mark 14:26-32), etc.

In Mark the Pharisees and some scribes from Jerusalem, the big city, notice that Jesus and his peasant associates did not wash their hands according to Pharisaic tradition before eating (7:3-5). On another occasion (Mark 2:23-28), the Pharisees pounced on Jesus because his disciples (who) were eating grain (what) as they walked through some else's grainfields (where). On yet another occasion (Mark 14:3-9), the chief priests and scribes lament the waste of costly perfume.

SIGNIFICANCE OF THE MEAL

As a ceremony, this final meal of Jesus with his disciples cements their mutual relationship. At this meal, Judas definitively separates himself from the group.

Jesus transforms the bread and wine into symbols of himself and the rescue he is about to effect for his friends and followers. The apostles would recognize that Jesus is performing what modern scholars call a "prophetic symbolic action," that is, an actual initiation of the event he is describing, namely, his redemptive death. Nevertheless, the disciples would not understand the complete meaning of the action until after the resurrection.

By interpreting Jesus' final meal as a Passover ceremony, the Synoptic evangelists added the dimension of "remembrance" to the event. A remembrance is a ceremony whose repetition would make present an event that occurred in the past. Each celebration of the Passover ceremony "makes present" that mighty salvific deed of God for the current generation. The same would now be true for subsequent generations of Christians who repeat and celebrate the Lord's Supper.

Knowing well the meaning of a meal enhances its observance.

Eleventh Sunday in Ordinary Time
Mark 4:26-34

Jesus seemed especially fond of using parables. In its form, the ancient Middle Eastern parable is a simile, that is, an explicit comparison of one item to another. Jesus' parables tell his listeners what God is like by comparing God's being or behavior to something familiar and known in the culture.

The reason why parables were and are difficult to interpret is because they point out how things are similar but also different. In other words, God is similar to, yet different from, whatever is presented as the point of comparison.

KINGDOM OF GOD

Many parables begin with the phrase "the kingdom of God is like . . .". The English phrase is unfortunate because Jesus is not describing a place (kingdom) but rather a person (God). Many scholars prefer to translate: "The reign of God is like . . .". In other words, a parable describes, or presents a scenario that illustrates what happens when God is totally in charge of life.

SEED

To understand the parable about the sown seed (vv. 26-29), a Western reader must be familiar with a very fundamental, ancient Middle Eastern conviction (common to all peasant societies): "All goods are finite in quantity, that is, limited in number, and already distributed." In other words, there is no more where this came from.

Any Middle Easterner who suddenly realized an increase in goods was considered a thief, because one peasant's gain usually meant another peasant's loss. Recall how the woman who lost a few coins rejoiced and invited friends to a party that cost more than the value of the rediscovered coins (Luke 15:8-9). It was imperative to demonstrate that she had not stolen the coins from another person or found what someone else had lost.

Yet peasants recognized certain yields, like livestock, a good crop, and children as exceptions. These increases were viewed as imponderable but very welcome gifts from God.

Even so, a limited-good culture expected that anyone who realized a sudden windfall should immediately share it with others rather than store it up for personal use in the future (see Luke 12:16-21). To keep it for one's personal benefit manifested greed.

In Mark's first parable today, the man is ignorant and perhaps even slothful. After planting the seed, he does nothing to help it along. He neither tills, weeds, nor irrigates the crop. Yet the earth itself brings forth the harvest.

What is God's reign like? If it depends upon human effort, one risks failure. If humans choose to trust God instead of relying upon themselves, unimaginable success can result. The choice is up to the one who hears the parable.

MUSTARD SEED

This parable presents a slight variation on the previous one. Mark makes the parable botanically correct: the mustard seed becomes a shrub, sometimes rather large, but it never grows into a tree (see Luke 13:19). Yet Mark notes that the shrub has large branches and that birds can make nests in its shade.

The listener is challenged to imagine how great the kingdom will be: will it be small and selective, only admitting a few? or will it look small (like a shrub) but actually be large enough to shelter varieties of birds?

The choice is up to the listener.

CONCLUSION

The puzzling remark about Jesus teaching the crowds in parables but explaining things in private to his disciples casts the parables into yet another light. To appreciate this light, a reader needs to understand the importance of secrecy in the ancient Mediterranean world.

Honor requires that outsiders should learn nothing damaging about insiders. Hence, secrecy is an important strategy for family groups. Yet it is also socially unacceptable because others will suspect that those who keep secrets are plotting to damage their honor. A troubling dilemma.

Jesus' parables spoken to the public (the outsiders) carry one meaning, but explained to his disciples (the insiders) carry another (e.g., compare the interpretation in Mark 4:10-20 to the parable in Mark 4:1-9).

Should the believer settle for the outsider interpretation or strive to gain the insider understanding? The choice is up to the listener!

Twelfth Sunday in Ordinary Time
Mark 4:35-41

Though contemporary Western believers read this story as a "miracle," first-century Mediterranean peasants would have seen that honor, the core value of that culture, permeates the story through and through.

FEAR

Mediterranean culture trains and expects males to behave bravely, especially in the face of danger. Nothing should ever shake the courage of a man. A public expression of fear is shameful.

Sirach (22:17-18) contrasts a firm resolution based on prudent understanding with a timid resolution based on foolish plans. He concludes that the latter will be unable to "withstand fear of any kind."

In today's gospel, there does not seem to have been any plan. At the end of the day Jesus suggested that he and his companions cross to the other side of the Sea of Galilee (v. 35). They depart, just as they are. Sudden and violent storms are common on this sea. Surely the men who sailed and fished there knew that.

That these experienced sailors and fishermen should yield to fear (see v. 40) is shameful and could be potentially damaging to their honor status if it ever became known to some outgroup like the people on either shore, or perhaps even to those in the other boats (v. 36). Jesus appears to "rub it in" by asking the embarrassing question, "Why are you afraid? Is your loyalty still weak?" (lit. "have you no faith," v. 40).

JESUS' POWER

Western readers of this story struggle to understand how a human being could control nature by word alone. Jesus' Middle Eastern contemporaries had no such problem. Rabbinic tradition speaks of people such as Honi the rain-making saint who challenged God to make it rain while he stood in a ring he drew on the ground (first century B.C.E., *Taanit* 24a), and Hanina ben Dosa who once caused a shower of rain to stop for his personal convenience and then begin again (*Taanit* 24b).

The first-century concern was not Jesus' power but the honor status that derived from this power. Peasants recognized an extensive hierarchy of spirits and people who possessed power to do things ordinary humans could not do. It was imperative to know where to rank such powerful beings in order to give them proper honor.

The disciples' question, "who then is this, that even sea and wind obey him?" (v. 41), is not an attempt to fathom Jesus' identity but rather to rank him properly in the honor hierarchy. Besides being more powerful than ordinary human beings, Jesus is also more powerful than sea and wind.

In the ancient world, anyone who behaved contrary to what was expected of their birth status (as Jesus seemed to do on a regular basis) posed a huge problem. Their power had to come from another source. The disciples' question about Jesus concerns the source of his extraordinary power.

In the case of Honi the rain-making saint, Simeon ben Shatah believed that he was clearly a spoilt child of God and therefore should be left alone rather than excommunicated for his irreverence toward God.

In the case of Jesus, opinion in the Gospels is mixed. Some, like the disciples in this story, are inclined to believe that he acted by the power of God, as he often claims. Others, like the scribes, believe that his power derives from the prince of demons (Mark 3:22).

FAITH = LOYALTY

In Western culture, and particularly the English language, faith or belief usually involves the psychological, internal, cognitive, and affective assent of the mind to truth. Such an understanding may well be present in Matthew 9:28 ("do you believe that I am able to do this?") and a few other passages. However, in the Middle Eastern world, the Hebrew and Greek words which are translated by the English word "faith" are better translated "personal loyalty" or "personal commitment."

In today's story, after Jesus stilled the storm he upbraided his disciples that fear of death shook their loyalty to him. Little did Jesus or any of the disciples realize how fear would again shake their loyalty to him later as he was arrested and led to certain death.

Thirteenth Sunday in Ordinary Time
Mark 5:21-43

Today's reading provides an excellent opportunity to reflect upon health and healing in the ancient Mediterranean world. Modern Western readers must suspend all that they know of the wonders of contemporary scientific medicine in order to enter a world where germs, microscopes, "cat scanners," and the impressive array of modern drugs were unknown.

THE HEMORRHAGING WOMAN

This woman suffered from her problem of menstrual irregularity for twelve years. Mark is often unfairly accused of physician bashing for his comment that she "suffered much under many physicians, spent all she had, and was no better but grew worse" (v. 26).

The ancient world knew at least two kinds of healers: professional physicians and folk healers. Mark tells us that until the moment she encountered Jesus, the hemorrhaging woman put all her trust and resources in professional physicians. Perhaps she was of elite status. Luke, who is very likely not a physician and probably not the one mentioned by Paul in Colossians 4:14, says the woman "could not be healed by anyone" (8:43).

Professional physicians hesitated to treat patients, because if the patient died the physician could be put to death too. They preferred to discuss illness (many were philosopher-physicians) and may well have offered this woman little more than philosophical reflection. In the New Testament, professional physicians are mentioned very infrequently (Mark 2:17 and parallels; 5:16; Luke 4:23; 8:43; Col 4:14) and chiefly in proverbs that were common in the ancient world.

Professional physicians in antiquity have little if anything in common with contemporary physicians. Because the Hebrews considered God to be their chief healer (Exod 15:26) they developed an ambivalent attitude toward professional physicians, as reflected in Sirach 38:1-23.

Folk healers in antiquity were much more commonly available to the peasants. They were willing to use their hands (John 9:6), touch people (Mark 8:22-26), and even risk failed treatments (Mark 6:5-6). In the gospel reports, people definitely identified Jesus as a folk healer, specifically a spirit-filled prophet who could still storms, conquer malevolent spirits, and restore people to their rightful and proper place in community.

In modern anthropological terms, we cannot know whether Jesus cured anyone because curing is directed toward disease (germs, viruses, and the like), and we have no evidence of the diseases his petitioners may have been suffering. Moreover, even in classical Greek literature, there is no indication that cures were expected to be permanent.

But in the same terms, Jesus definitely healed all who wanted to be healed. Healing is the restoration of meaning to people's lives no matter what their physical condition might be. Curing is very rare, but healing takes place infallibly, 100 percent of the time, because sooner or later all people regain meaning in life and resume their rightful place in society.

This is certainly what Jesus accomplished for the hemorrhaging woman. Her condition rendered her ritually unclean and not only prevented her from entering the Temple but also required that she remove herself from the community, the equivalent of social death in the Mediterranean world.

Notice that Jesus sometimes is unaware of and has no control over his power (see v. 39). The woman evoked it without his awareness or permission. Nevertheless, Jesus declares what he and the woman know has occurred: "the condition no longer exists; welcome back to the community, daughter!"

THE DEAD TEENAGER

In the first century, 60 percent of live births usually died by their mid-teens. The scene presented here was a very common one.

Like other ancient healers, Jesus sometimes used a formula. The fact that the Greek Gospel retains Jesus' Aramaic words "Talitha cum" ("little girl, get up") reflects the ancient belief that power is in the original words and not the translation. Some associate this with magic.

The crowd's laughter at Jesus' claim that the girl is only sleeping challenges his honor. Jesus' command that the family say nothing is his way of getting even with the crowd. They'll never know what happened.

As proof that the girl is healed, that is, restored to her rightful place in community, Jesus commands that she eat with her family. Jesus the healer restores meaning to life and returns people to communal solidarity.

Fourteenth Sunday in Ordinary Time
Mark 6:1-6

Honor governs every dimension of life in the Mediterranean world. This is particularly evident in today's reading, where Jesus is "in his own country," that is, Nazareth or the vicinity.

INHERITED HONOR

One's basic claim to honor derives from birth and is determined by the circumstances of birth. Technically, this is called ascribed honor. In today's episode, the people are fully aware of Jesus' "ascribed honor." "Is this not the carpenter, the son of Mary and brother of James and Joses and Judas and Simon, and are not his sisters here with us?" These family members help identify Jesus' honor rating.

Of particular interest in this list is the statement that Jesus is "the son of Mary." In the Middle East, a son is always identified by the father (e.g., Simon bar [= son of] Jonah; James and John, the sons of Zebedee). Identifying a son by the mother's name usually signals some confusion about the father. Luke (4:22) corrects Mark's report and removes any hint of scandal by identifying Jesus as "Joseph's son."

A second important point is the crowd's identification of Jesus' status: an artisan. In the Middle East, a son is expected to take up his father's occupation or profession. There is no expectation of "doing better than one's parents" or "getting ahead in life." Honor requires that persons remain in their inherited status and make no effort to improve on it.

ACHIEVED HONOR

Teaching in the synagogue was permissible to qualified males. Jesus' teaching is so impressive that people were astonished by his words. "Many who heard him were astonished" by his teaching and moved by his mighty deeds (v. 2). They seemed ready to grant the honor Jesus was claiming by his striking teaching.

But the crowd, the ultimate judge and bestower of achieved honor, stops short and refuses to concur. To begin with, Jesus is recognized as a craftsman, that is, a worker in wood (scarce and precious in ancient Palestine) and stone (more plentiful than wood). Craftsmen at that time, especially those who lived in hamlets like Nazareth, had to leave home to find work. This means they left their women (wives, mothers, sisters) at home without requisite male protection to safeguard the family's honor. For this reason, craftsmen were viewed as persons "without shame," that is, without sufficient sensitivity to the requirements of honor.

Secondly, where could a person born to a manual craftsman gain such astounding wisdom? Even more, how could a craftsman presumably busy at his craft ever obtain such wisdom? "And they took offense at him" (v. 3; compare Sir 38:24–39:5).

JESUS' RIPOSTE

The Gospels indicate that Jesus was a shrewd man of his culture. He could readily size up a situation and respond with a perfectly appropriate comment. In the vast majority of instances, the perfectly appropriate comment is an insult. Throughout the Gospels, Jesus demonstrates that he is a master of insult.

Anticipating that the crowd is not going to grant him honor, Jesus takes the offensive. He quotes a proverb to those who wanted to shame him: "A prophet is not without honor, except in his own country, and among his own kin, and in his own house" (v. 4). With one fell swoop Jesus insults his neighbors, his relatives, and his family. He shames them before they can shame him.

His point is that outsiders are better able to determine the honor rating of a prophet, one who speaks the will of God for the here and now, than insiders, the people who should know him best. Mark does not tell us how the crowd responded, but we can well guess that Luke's report is on target. They were so enraged that they wanted to kill him (4:29).

Because Jesus' neighbors, relatives, and family could not extend to him emotion-filled loyalty, commitment, and solidarity ("faith" in traditional translations), he could not perform for them the mighty works he did for others. Self-inflicted problems are the worst.

Fifteenth Sunday in Ordinary Time
Mark 6:7-13

Jesus gathers his faction (the Twelve) and sends them out with authority over unclean spirits. This is an astonishing authorization which moves these Twelve up a notch in their honor status.

SPIRITS

People in the ancient Mediterranean world not only held a strong belief in the existence of spirits but also ranked them according to power. At the top of the list was "our" God, then "other" gods, sons of god, or archangels. In third place were still less powerful nonhuman persons: angels, spirits, and demons. Humans were in fourth place, and creatures lower than humans in last place.

By giving the Twelve power over unclean spirits, Jesus moves them up from level four at least into level three. Greeks called hostile spirits "demons," while Semites called them "unclean spirits." When Jesus expels an unclean spirit (Mark 5:2, 8) out of a possessed man in pagan territory, the people of that region call the man a demoniac (Mark 5:15-16).

Modern believers tend to call this activity "exorcism," but the New Testament does not use this word. The entire consideration is rather based on "authority" or "power." Jesus has authority over unclean spirits, and the Gospel writers frequently note that his success in expelling unclean spirits is evidence for his authority. Notice in today's reading that

Jesus shares this authority with the Twelve (v. 7) and they cast out many demons (v. 13).

HEALING

The authority over unclean spirits also extends to conditions believed to be caused by these spirits, namely, sickness. That the distinction between possession and sickness is fuzzy in the ancient world is evident in the story of Peter's mother-in-law. In Mark (1:30) she is "sick with a fever," but the context of Luke (4:38-39) indicates that the "high fever" that grips her is actually a demon named "Fever" whom Jesus "rebukes" and expels.

TRAVEL AND HOSPITALITY

In the ancient world, travel was deviant and dangerous. It was deviant because there was little reason to leave one's ancestral dwelling where one was normally surrounded by extended family network. Everything one needed or desired was here. It was dangerous because robbers waited to ambush travellers, particularly those travelling alone (Luke 10:30). For this reason, Jesus tells his newly authorized faction members to travel in pairs. Very likely these pairs joined larger caravans for greater safety.

The instruction to travel lightly (no bread, no money, etc.) is not unusual. The needs of travellers (lodging and food) were to be provided chiefly through hospitality. Jesus continues his instruction with special attention to hospitality (e.g., "receiving" or "welcoming").

In the Middle Eastern world, hospitality is a value extended exclusively to strangers. (Relatives and friends are extended steadfast loving kindness.) The process involves three steps: the stranger is taken under the protection of a host for a given time, transformed into a temporary guest, with hopes that the two will part friends (but parting as enemies is also possible).

The host provides lodging, food, and especially a safe haven or protection from the suspicions and possible attacks of villagers. After all, strangers are always suspected of being up to no good and plotting damage to the village.

Failure to extend hospitality in the Middle East is a serious breach of honor. Jesus' advice to "shake off the dust on your feet as a testimony against those who would not extend hospitality" is a major insult. It effectively writes these people out of the human community. The gesture implied total rejection, hostility, and an unwillingness to be touched by anything the others have touched.

These culturally different understandings of spirits, travel, and hospitality challenge Western believers to gain a well-founded grasp of Middle Eastern culture. Contemporary books about angels and other spirits tend to reflect modern Western theological or spiritual concepts that sometimes have slim foundation in the Middle Eastern biblical texts. A sound, cross-cultural approach to reading and understanding the Bible can lay a much stronger foundation for the commendable exploration of these traditional topics.

Sixteenth Sunday in Ordinary Time
Mark 6:30-34

The image of a "lonely" place (vv. 31, 32) painted in today's reading prepares for Mark's next story, about the feeding of five thousand. But the image is worth pondering for fresh insights it can give into our Mediterranean ancestors in the faith.

In the New Testament, the Greek word translated "lonely" or "deserted" and used with "place" basically describes an uninhabited region or one with a very small population. The word can also describe a place of sparse vegetation. Although the two ideas are related, the New Testament usage applies more often to population.

In first-century Palestine, there were fewer than three or four large cities like Jerusalem. Ninety percent of the population lived outside the large cities in hamlets or villages with a small number of residents. The population of Nazareth may not have been more than 150 and could have been as small as 50. Try to imagine "privacy" in a settlement of this size!

These small settlements were not packed densely close to each other. There was a significant distance between them, and this uninhabited space was generally viewed as chaos or "a lonely place." The modern experience of "a family picnic in the park" simply could and did not occur in the first-century Mediterranean world.

Jesus' suggestion that he and his disciples, freshly returned from their journey, leave his neighborhood (Nazareth) and go off to a lonely place is well explained by the next sentence: "Many were coming and going, and they had no leisure even to eat" (v. 31). If Jesus is still in his own country (Mark 6:1), then he and his disciples are well known to everybody. In the Middle East, everybody minds everybody else's business. Privacy is practically nonexistent. Rest is all but impossible. And if anyone is eating, it would be impolite and inconsiderate not to share with others.

Western readers given to fast-food outlets and the tendency to eat on the run might even miss the significance of Jesus' remark about "no leisure even to eat." All meals in the Mediterranean world are leisurely events. Even more important than the nourishment, meals provide opportunities for strengthening personal bonds between those at table. Since the disciples were away from Jesus for a while, it was important to renew the bonds between then. What better way to do it than with a leisurely meal? So it was quite likely that Jesus and the Twelve took food with them which they could not eat in leisure in his neighborhood. Perhaps it was the five loaves and two fish that appear at the feeding of the multitude (Mark 6:38).

Yet the nosey crowds give Jesus and his followers no rest. Mark presents a humorous picture. "Many saw them going, and knew them, and they ran there on foot from all the towns, and got there ahead of them" (Mark 6:33). It is not just that they "saw them," but some were certainly keeping an eye on them.

Any group going off to a lonely place raised suspicions. What did they have to hide? What are they up to? Why are they being secretive? Who goes off to uninhabited places known to be rife with demons and wild beasts? If nosey people wanted to stay "in the know," they had to run to get to the boat's landing place even before the vessel arrived.

Jesus' response to them is compassion (v. 34) because they were like "sheep without a shepherd." The Hebrew word for "compassion" derives from the word for "womb." In the Middle East, compassion is considered a female value and virtue.

Sheep are basically dumb animals. No one can lead them; they have to be driven. Without a shepherd, sheep simply lie down and don't move ahead. Jesus perceives that the people have basic needs that are going unmet. Moved to compassion for them, Jesus teaches the great throng many things sufficiently interesting and engaging to keep them there dangerously late. Being in an uninhabited place far from kin and without provisions, everyone wondered: what's next? The story continues in the next weeks.

Seventeenth Sunday in Ordinary Time
John 6:1-15

Scholars recognize that John did not copy his account of the feeding of the crowds from the Synoptics but rather worked from an independent tradition. His account contains some very ancient elements as well as creative elaborations of details found in his sources.

One example of an ancient or perhaps "original" element is Jesus' question to Philip: "How are we to buy bread, so that these people may eat?" (v. 5). That Jesus' apparent ignorance about this was embarrassing to the early Christians is evident in the editorial comment that follows: "he said this to test him, for he himself knew what he would do."

An example of creative elaboration is in verses 11-12 which carry clear Eucharistic overtones and quite likely depended on the Synoptic account of the institution of the Eucharist, a tradition not included in John's passion story.

SYNAGOGUE READINGS

To appreciate John's creative elaboration of tradition, it is helpful to reflect upon a hypothesis proposed years ago by Aileen Guilding. She attempted to reconstruct a three-year cycle of Scripture readings in the synagogue. The first reading was from the Torah (Genesis, Exodus, Leviticus, Numbers and Deuteronomy). An accompanying reading, the *haphtarah*, was taken from the Prophets. (Others think a third reading may have been later drawn from the Psalms. Three years of readings amounted to 150 selections and there are 150 psalms.)

In the Gospel traditions about Jesus feeding the people, only John mentions the calendrical time of the event. "Now the Passover, the feast of the Judeans, was at hand" (v. 4). The story of Jesus feeding the people seems to echo the story of God feeding his people in the Exodus with manna and quail (Exod 16).

In Guilding's reconstruction of the synagogue lectionary, Exodus was read in cycle 2, and Exodus 11–16 would be read during the six weeks after Pentecost. The *haphtarah* reading at the same time would be Isaiah 54–55, and Isaiah 54 is quoted in John 6:45. Guilding hypothesizes that it was these synagogue readings at Passover time that provided early Christians with ideas for creating the Johannine story of Jesus feeding a large crowd of people.

Many disagree with her view that the story is fictional. But the parallels and relationships she highlights make it plausible that the synagogue readings may well have contributed to the creation of the discourse Jesus delivered after the feeding. John notes: "This he [Jesus] said in the synagogue, as he taught in Capernaum" (v. 59). Jesus himself may have drawn on the lectionary themes to develop his discourse.

BREAD AND FISH

The people are fed with bread and fish. John specifies barley loaves. Barley was the most common grain after wheat. It manages to survive extreme heat as well as water shortages much better than wheat. Moreover, it ripens in less time. Since the feast of Passover coincides with the barley harvest, the presence of barley loaves in this story makes plausible sense.

The Greek word for "fish" here derives from another word that means "food that is cooked and eaten with bread." The idea is that the fish is not fresh but already prepared, or, more correctly, processed. Rabbinic sources indicate that fish were processed for preservation and transportation in a variety of forms: cured, pickled, salted, or dried. And wine would sometimes be mixed in with fish-brine. In John's story, the fish are most likely dried or preserved.

Scholars wonder why Jesus should single out Philip to ask, "Where shall we ever buy bread for these people to eat?" Philip indicates that he is not unaware of the challenge because in his experienced judgment, two hundred days' wages couldn't buy enough loaves to feed the crowd.

Philip was from Bethsaida, which was the capital of Gaulanitis. Located on the northern shore of the Sea of Galilee, the village's name means "fishing village" (Mark 6:45). Therefore, if this scene takes place in Bethsaida (as Luke suggests), then Philip is exactly the one to ask. He would be most familiar with local conditions.

Background information about synagogue lectionaries, local geography, and food and fish help contemporary believers to appreciate how much they need to know about ancient culture in order to begin to interpret the Scripture respectfully.

Eighteenth Sunday in Ordinary Time
John 6:24-35

The highlight of this passage is faith, or more precisely as John states it: "believing in Jesus." The fourth evangelist uses this phrase thirty-four times, indicating that it has special meaning for him.

FAITH

This word appears often in the Bible and is frequently mentioned by believers. As with all words and with human language itself, meaning derives basically and primarily from the society that uses the word. In the United States, faith or belief has a strong intellectual character. It is considered primarily to be an act of the mind.

Furthermore, faith usually indicates (to Americans) that a person believes something or someone on the basis of authority. Thus, any person, including an actor or impostor, who wears a white laboratory coat with a stethoscope tucked into its pocket is thought to be "believable."

Actors playing physicians on American television became so influential in past years that prestigious medical schools used to invite them as commencement speakers. Scientific medicine recognizes that in the final analysis, all healing is faith healing. Whatever a person believes can be effective. This is the basis for the placebo effect.

"BELIEVING IN(TO)"

In the Middle Eastern world, the words "faith," "belief," "fidelity," and "faithfulness" describe the social glue that binds one person to another person. These are not acts of the mind so much as sentiments that spring from the heart, the seat of thought in Middle Eastern psychology.

These terms really describe the social, externally manifested, emotionally rooted values known as loyalty, commitment, and solidarity. John underlines this aspect (rather than the intellectual one) by his favorite phrase: "believing in" or "into" Jesus.

In today's episode, people come looking for Jesus but for the wrong reason: they don't want to miss out if he is going to offer more to eat (v. 26). Given the subsistence diet on which first century peasants lived, one might say Jesus was very insensitive to scold them for seeking him because he fed them. Jesus tried to move their thoughts from perishable food to that which "endures to eternal life which the Son of Man will give to you." Yet it is difficult to think lofty thoughts when one's stomach growls from hunger.

The people understand Jesus' point and ask a follow up question. "What works of God ought we do in order to gain this sustenance?" (v. 28). Qumran literature indicates that the phrase "works of God" describes those things that please God. People should do these and avoid what is displeasing.

According to Jesus, what truly pleases God is to "believe in him whom God has sent" (v. 29). This is not simply intellectual assent, but authentic Mediterranean commitment, loyalty, and solidarity. Stick with Jesus no matter what!

If the people sound as if they are making headway in understanding Jesus, their next statement indicates just how much further they have yet to travel. They ask Jesus for a sign to authenticate himself. This was, of course, normal in the tradition. A true prophet must legitimate himself and his announcement with a sign.

Thinking of the great prophet, Moses, the people ask Jesus for a sign like manna. How quickly they have forgotten about the bread which he gave just the day before. Jesus, of course, has already noted that these people missed the point of the bread—"sign" (v. 26) because their minds were elsewhere.

He corrects their understanding of Exodus 16:15: it was not Moses but God who gave and continues to give bread from heaven. Now, Jesus not only gives the bread of life (John 6:11, 27) but also is the bread of life (John 6:35, 48). The giver and the gift are one and the same.

The parallel structure of Jesus' concluding comment expresses a synonym for John's favorite phrase, "believing into." "He who *comes to* me shall not hunger, he who *believes in* me shall never thirst" (v. 35). Other synonyms are "abide with," "follow," "love," "keep the words of," "receive," "have," and "see." All of these underscore the need for believers to establish commitment and solidarity with Jesus, the bread of life.

Nineteenth Sunday in Ordinary Time
John 6:41-51

American cultural heroes invariably include the person of humble origins who rises to achieve great status. Abraham Lincoln is but one familiar example. That such achievement is possible is a corollary of the American cultural belief in the equality of all persons. When real experience belies this belief, Americans fall back on the idea of equal opportunity. At least, every one can rise to a greater position than the one that came with birth.

Such a notion is entirely lacking in the ancient Mediterr anean world. Basic honor derives from birth into very specific circumstances. Honor requires that a person remain in this status, maintain and preserve it, and never consider "getting ahead." Any attempt to improve upon or behave not in keeping with one's birth status is shameful because it is a divisive force in community.

CONFLICT OF INTERPRETATIONS

Even as the listeners are impressed by Jesus' teaching and marvel at the themes he develops from the Scripture read in the synagogue for the season of Passover, the application he makes to himself is jarring. It causes them to murmur.

The Greek word for "murmur" that appears here is the same one that appears in the Greek translation of the Hebrew Scriptures when they describe the murmuring of the

121

Israelites during the Exodus (Exod 16:2, 7, 8). This associational allusion is a masterful piece of artistry.

Even more striking is the critical complaint that erupts over the interpretation of Exodus 16! Earlier (6:31) the people put forth their interpretation, which Jesus corrected (6:32, 35). They are skeptical of Jesus' interpretation and voice their concern in typical Mediterranean fashion. They attack Jesus for stepping outside of his inherited honorable status (vv. 42-43).

The demonstrative pronoun in the phrase "Isn't this Jesus . . . ?" (v. 42) implies a disrespectful tone and would be appropriately translated as "this fellow" or "this chap." The people recite Jesus' inherited status: son of Joseph; they know full well the honor-ratings of his father and mother. Parents and family of origin constitute one's claim to basic honor. The claim "to have come down from heaven" (6:32) is audacious, incredible, and threatening to an established and well-ordered community. How dare Jesus claim more honor than he deserves?

Scholars suggest that the word "murmur" among interpreters of the Torah in Jesus' world indicated a disagreement with another interpretation of the Scripture. The disagreement is expressed in a sentence beginning with "how." Clearly the people disagree with Jesus' interpretation of Scripture and his application of it to himself. Jesus' response is quite direct: "Stop your murmuring."

CONTEMPORARY INTERPRETATION

As is often the case in John's Gospel, communication is going on at many levels. The Church reminds Bible readers to distinguish the meaning a passage might have had in Jesus' lifetime from the meaning it could have had at the time of the evangelist.

The discussion in John 6:35-50 very plausibly reflects the lifetime of Jesus. No mention is made of eating the bread until verse 51. Bread in the Old Testament frequently represents divine instruction. In verse 45 Jesus quotes loosely from Isaiah 54:13: "They shall all be taught by God." Thus the point that would be understood in Jesus' day is that the instruction Jesus gives about the Father is life-yielding bread for those who believe in him whom God has sent.

The idea of eating the bread which emerges and becomes strong in verses 51-58 is likely the product of early Christian insight, now placed on Jesus' lips. Yet it is also a secondary theme in verses 35-50. In other words, while modern Bible readers recognize the creative work of the evangelists in the Gospels, much of it is rooted in the life of the historical Jesus himself.

Over the last fifty years and more, the Church has given scholars and believers an impressive set of guidelines for respectfully reading and interpreting the Gospels. The reflections above are drawn from scholars who reached their conclusions with the aid of these guidelines. A respectful interpretation of Scripture is very demanding but very rewarding.

Ninety-five percent of the population of Jesus' time was illiterate, but their familiarity with Scripture made for heated discussions. This should encourage a contemporary Christian to learn the guidelines and master the Scriptures.

Twentieth Sunday
in Ordinary Time
John 6:51-58

EUCHARIST

Anyone who reads these verses carefully cannot help but notice the strong and explicit Eucharistic tone. The question then arises: could Jesus have spoken such words in the middle of his ministry? Prior to the Last Supper, how could anyone—crowd or disciples—understand or appreciate Eucharistic interpretations? The verses as they appear in the Gospel, therefore, were likely not spoken in this form by Jesus.

Yet, everyone who reads the Gospel of John knows that while he devotes five chapters (13–17) to the Last Supper, his narrative does not include the institution of the Eucharist. For this and other reasons, scholars believe that the multiplication of loaves and the discourse in chapter 6 are John's equivalent of an institution narrative.

Are these verses a pure creation by the evangelist? The Church's guidelines for interpreting the Scriptures admit that the evangelists sometimes creatively reported the tradition they received about Jesus. "From the many things handed down they selected some things, reduced others to a synthesis, (still) others they explicated as they kept in mind the situation of the churches" (*Historical Truth of the Gospels,* no. 9).

On the basis of these guidelines and further research, Catholic scholars do not believe that verses 51-58 are the result of the evangelist's creative imagination (unlike the story of doubting Thomas). They could plausibly have been part of

Jesus' reflection on readings heard in the Synagogue during the Passover season, but the Eucharistic overtones were probably the result of Christian rethinking of this topic added at a late stage in the final edition of the Fourth Gospel.

The objection "How can this man give us his flesh to eat?" (v. 52) is serious and would likely have arisen in Jesus' lifetime. The problem was no less real in the time of the evangelist, sixty years later. Literal drinking of blood was prohibited in Judaism and perhaps also in early Christianity (see Gen 9:4; Lev 17:10, 12, 14; cf. Acts 15:29).

Yet "eating Jesus' flesh and drinking his blood" became a common way for Christians around the time of John's Gospel to describe participation in the Eucharist. Ignatius of Antioch said, "I desire 'the bread of God' which is the flesh of Jesus Christ . . . and for drink I desire his blood" (*Romans* 7.3).

The Johannine scholar Charles H. Talbert believes that such language serves to describe intimacy, the close relationship of Jesus to those who believe in him, or who place their commitment and loyalty in him. Thus, the Father has life in himself (John 5:26), and so too does the Son (ibid.), and so too do believers who share an intimate relationship with Jesus by sharing in the sacrament of the Eucharist.

Talbert continues and highlights the distinctive contribution John's thinking makes to Christian theology. In John's view, the Eucharist is not so much a memorial of Jesus' death (see 1 Cor 11:23-25) nor a continuation of mealtimes with Jesus during his life and after his resurrection (Luke 24:13-35). Rather, John views the Eucharist as a liturgical or cultic extension of Jesus' incarnation. This is why, according to Talbert, John placed Jesus' Eucharistic words at this moment, the middle of his public ministry, immediately after his lengthy "homily" on the nourishment he provides in revealing the Father.

This illustrates the Church's guidelines which note: "Let the interpreter seek out the meaning intended by the Evangelist in narrating a saying or deed in a certain way or in placing it in a certain context. For the truth of the story is not at all affected by the fact that the Evangelists related the words and deeds of our Lord in a different order, and express His sayings not literally but differently" (*Historical Truth of the Gospels*, no. 9)

John's Gospel is a favorite of many believers, but few ever plumb the depths of his masterpiece. It takes careful reading, intense study, and prayerful reflection to tune correctly into John's wavelength. The clear sound that emerges from such effort is nothing less than heavenly.

Twenty-First Sunday in Ordinary Time
John 6:60-69

COMMITMENT AND FACTIONS

In a late spring issue of a student newspaper published at a prestigious Catholic university, the graduating editor reflected on things he was glad he had done. Number two on his list was leaving the Catholic Church. Already as a freshman, he knew that for moral reasons he could not remain part of the Church and be true "to all the values I believed in."

The scene in today's gospel is not quite parallel to this student's situation, but there is a small similarity. Here in the middle of Jesus' ministry, just after an extraordinary reflection on the synagogue readings, the listeners are divided. Some react negatively: "This is a hard saying; who can listen to it?" (v. 60). Others desert him: "Many of his disciples drew back and no longer went about with him" (v. 66).

Jesus reminds those who are taken aback that though the manna was a gift from heaven, it belonged to the realm of life on earth. It was a temporary aid with no use beyond its time. The words Jesus has spoken to them (6:35-58) are "spirit and life" (v. 63). They put the believer in touch with the Spirit and therefore with life at its source.

Jesus knew that there were some among his listeners who were not loyal to him, would refuse to have solidarity with him ("there are some of you who do not believe," v. 64). There was even one that would prove to be totally disloyal, aloof, and not deeply committed to Jesus and his group (the one who would betray him). Faith, loyalty, commitment, and solidarity are gifts. "No one can come to me unless it is granted him by the Father" (v. 65).

Those who deserted Jesus certainly disappointed him, but to a faction founder such desertion would be serious only if the core group, the Twelve, deserted him. He asks them point-blank: "Will you also go away?" (v. 67). Speaking on behalf of the faction, Simon Peter responds, "Lord, to whom shall we go? You have the words of eternal life and we have believed, and have come to know, that you are the Holy One of God" (v. 68).

Peter's response translated into Mediterranean cultural values is: we have made a commitment to you, no matter what ("we have believed"). Identifying Jesus as the "Holy One of God" echoes the Old Testament use of this phrase to identify men consecrated to God. Samson was so described (Judg 13:7; 16:7), as was Aaron (Ps 106:16). In John 10:36, Jesus describes himself as "the one whom the Father made holy," and in John 17:19, Jesus says, "It is for them [my disciples] that I make myself holy."

Peter thinks he speaks for the Twelve, but Jesus knows better. Actually, any Mediterranean person would know better. In the Mediterranean world, allegiance between each member of a faction and its leader is strong. The leader has recruited each member personally and individually.

But the allegiance between faction members is very weak. If they know each other at all, it is only superficially. They have no in-depth psychological insight into other persons. Moreover, they could care less about the other faction members. James and John, the sons of Zebedee, approach Jesus to seek higher honors than the other ten when Jesus enters into the fullness of his rightful honor (Mark 10:37). The others become understandably indignant (an understatement in view of the typical Mediterranean penchant for venting emotions).

Jesus' observation that one of the Twelve is "a devil" may well have come from the hand of the editor who adds his after-the-fact comment: "He spoke of Judas the son of Simon Iscariot, for he, one of the twelve, was to betray him." Mediterranean people generally judge others only on externals (see 1 Sam 16:7).

Those who abandoned Jesus in today's story choose to remain faithful to another set of values. Some who stayed with him did not fully understand Jesus and his values. One betrayed him, another denied him, and all abandoned him. The ultimate question may well be, by whose values will we live?

Twenty-Second Sunday in Ordinary Time
Mark 7:1-8, 14-15, 21-23

CONFLICT

In an honor-based culture, conflict is unavoidable. All males must engage either in public display of honor or in challenges to the honor claims of others. The Pharisees and their scholars ("scribes") routinely spy on Jesus and his disciples in order to challenge their growing honorable reputation. In this reading, they challenge Jesus' disciples' failure to observe "The Great Tradition."

TRADITION

The "tradition of the elders" (v. 5) is described by modern anthropologists as "The Great Tradition," that is, a set of practices defined, maintained, and practiced by elites who lived in the cities. The Pharisees required that everyone observe this urban tradition. Peasants in the countryside, or itinerants like Jesus and his followers, would have difficulty observing this tradition. Water was scarce and/or not readily available for ablutions, and fishermen routinely came into contact with dead fish, dead animals, and other pollutants.

Peasants therefore developed "The Little Tradition" which adapted requirements of "The Great Tradition" to the realities and deficiencies of peasant life. Jesus the artisan not only sided with "The Little Tradition" but hurled a counterchallenge to the Pharisees for minimizing and ignoring the Law of Moses in preference for their "Great Tradition" (Mark 7:9-13).

STRATEGY

The process we can observe in today's reading is technically called "challenge and riposte." Few questions in the Mediterranean world are innocuous. Every question is a challenge, if for no other reason than that the addressee might not know the answer and be shamed or forced to lie.

The question the Pharisees direct to Jesus concerns the way in which his disciples eat: they do not ritually purify their hands (wash) before eating (v. 5).

Jesus' response here is typical of his every response to a challenge. He invariably replies with an insult. In this instance he calls the Pharisees "hypocrites." The Greek word *hypokrites* means "actor." An appropriate way to render Jesus' insult in English would be: "You actors! Scripture may be the lines you quote, but is it not the script by which you live."

Then Jesus typically quotes or refers to Scripture. Here he quotes Isaiah 29:13 against his opponents. It was an especially honorable skill for a male to be able to draw creatively upon tradition in the heat of conflict or a discussion. The Pharisees hoped to shame Jesus, but Jesus shames them instead by insulting them, quoting Scripture creatively, and hurling a counterchallenge: they value their human tradition much more than the Torah, the Law of Moses.

Next Jesus changes the topic, a strategy he frequently uses in conflict situations. The Pharisees asked about "the way" the disciples ate (with ritually defiled hands). Jesus changes the topic to "what" disciples might eat, that is, defiling and nondefiling foods (v. 15).

THE CROWD

Because publicity is the essential hallmark of honor-claims and challenges, the crowd plays a critical role. The text does not explicitly say that the crowd sided with Jesus, but the context appears to indicate that they did. In the crowd's judgment, Jesus won this skirmish with the Pharisees.

TODAY'S GOSPEL

At this point in the story, the architects of the Lectionary have manipulated the gospel text and changed the evangelist's setting. According to Mark, Jesus' statement about defiling and nondefiling foods is a "parable." He meant what he said but also intended something other and something more.

In Mark, the further explanation is given to the disciples and not to the crowd. For some reason, today's Lectionary reading passes over an element of secrecy which characterizes both Mark's Gospel and Mediterranean society in general. Unlike the United States, in the Mediterranean world no one has "the right to know" anything. It's simply none of your business.

Americans are dismayed by Jesus' preference for confrontation and conflict rather than dialogue and his reliance upon insult instead of tact and diplomacy. By changing the topic of the conflict, Jesus manipulates the situation to his advantage. Does Jesus present a good model to imitate? How might a believer rewrite this scene to fit American values?

Twenty-Third Sunday in Ordinary Time
Mark 7:31-37

DEAF AND MUTE

The Greek word often translated as "deaf" may sometimes mean "mute." Indeed in Matthew 11:5 and Luke 7:22, the deaf are made to hear, while in Matthew 9:32; 12:22; and Luke 11:14, the deaf are made to speak. The association of both meanings with one Greek word is understandable because the two skills are related. Speaking involves the ability to imitate what one hears.

In this story, Mark intends the meaning "deaf" since he adds another very specific Greek word that means "unable to speak properly." That this man could speak at all suggests he may not have been congenitally deaf, or that his hearing loss was not total.

JESUS' HEALING ACTIVITY

First, Jesus takes the man aside "in private." Given the very public and nosey nature of Mediterranean culture, privacy is practically impossible. Also, people tend to stand very close to each other. Touching or leaning against other people is not at all a problem. What Jesus did here was gain some elbow-room or breathing space for himself and his client.

Second, given the readiness of people in this culture to touch and make contact with others, Jesus' laying on of hands does not have the significance it might have in antiseptic and aloof Western culture. In antiquity, the hands were the customary vehicle by which a healer transmitted therapeutic power to the client. At other times, the healer's garments transmitted healing power without the healer's awareness or will (Mark 5:28-29). Sometimes the healer could be effective at a distance by word alone (Luke 7:7).

Third, spitting is a common Middle Eastern precaution against evil. A person who suspects another of possessing or casting the "evil eye" will spit to deflect or deactivate that power. The Galatians "spit" when they saw Paul whom they suspected of having an "evil eye" (Gal 4:14, literal translation). Traditional healers routinely use this strategy to ward off evil.

Fourth, Mark is careful to report the precise Aramaic word used by Jesus: *'eppattah,* or as reported in English translations, *ephphatha.* The ancients believed that words contain power. If translated, the word would lose its power. By reporting the original Aramaic word, Mark underscores Jesus' power as a traditional healer. (See Thirteenth Sunday above, raising the dead teenager.)

The result: immediately the man's ears were opened, the bond of his tongue was released, and he spoke properly or plainly.

HONOR

Once again Jesus ordered the crowd to tell no one, but the more he ordered them the more zealously they proclaimed it. An earlier generation of scholars identified this strange injunction as part of "the messianic secret" in Mark's Gospel. Contemporary scholars point out that the issue is much more complex.

To begin with, in the first century of the common era, there was no single, uniform, widely accepted concept of who the Messiah would be and what he was expected to accomplish. There were, rather, so many conflicting and contradictory notions of the Messiah that keeping it a secret need imply no deep purpose; it would simply be a relief. One less puzzle to deal with.

Second, honor requires that each person remain within the bonds of honor deriving from birth-status. With his travels and healing activity, Jesus has stepped outside the bounds of his honor rating and now poses a serious threat to his culture. As an honorable man, he must do his utmost to keep this potentially damaging information hidden from public awareness.

Third, the most common strategy for safeguarding the honor of Jesus' family is secrecy, deception, and lying. By urging secrecy on his benefactors, Jesus could continue his ministry to the benefit of everyone including his family, kin, and neighbors. In the long run, of course, it didn't work.

Scientifically sophisticated Western believers would prefer to debate whether or not the man "really" was deaf and tongue-tied in order to discern "scientifically" what Jesus really did. None of this was of interest in antiquity. Whatever "really" happened, Jesus restored meaning to his clients' lives. That is what healing means. What fresh meaning can this episode add to the life of a modern believer?

Twenty-Fourth Sunday in Ordinary Time
Mark 8:27-35

In the thirteenth century, Francis of Assisi had a vision of Jesus Christ hanging on the cross and grasped the meaning of the gospel passage: "If any want to become my followers, let them deny themselves and take up their cross and follow me" (Mark 8:34 and parallels). Shortly thereafter when his father summoned him before Bishop Guido of Assisi to renounce all claims to inheritance, Francis went even further and severed ties with his father. "Until now I called you my father, but from now on I can say without reservation, 'Our Father who art in heaven.'"

What prompted the Italian Francis to interpret "denying oneself" as "denying one's father and family?" The Mediterranean cultural understanding of "self" as a communal rather than an individualistic identity lay at the foundation of Francis' mindset.

TAKING UP THE CROSS

In the Synoptic "triple tradition" (Mark 8:34; Matt 16:24; Luke 9:23), Jesus' statement is constructed in this way:

    A - follow me;
    B - deny oneself;
    B' - take up cross;
    A' - follow me.

Phrases A and A' are identical or synonymous. So too are phrases B and B'. Therefore, to take up one's cross means to deny oneself.

In the "double tradition" (Matt 10:34-38; Luke 14:25-27), taking up one's cross is associated with denial of one's family or kin. This cluster of matching passages informs the discerning reader that taking up one's cross is equivalent to denying oneself (triple tradition) and to denying one's family or kin group (double tradition).

MEDITERRANEAN PERSONALITY

Crosscultural specialists underscore the contrast between Western and Mediterranean notions of personality and the self. In Western culture, people develop a keen sense of individualism, self-reliance, independence from others, and personal competence.

In the Middle East, people are urged to focus primarily on the family and forge their identity according to the family. Simon Peter is known as son of Jonah; Jesus is the carpenter's or Mary's son. Middle Easterners depend upon the family for everything. Indeed, the rule is "take care of family first." In modern Middle Eastern countries, a royal family exclusively hires relatives as government servants. People in these cultures always feel the need of forming a coalition to achieve anything. No one dares to dream of personal initiative.

From a social-psychological perspective, Western individualists care nothing about what others may say or think of them and their behavior. They march to the beat of a different drummer and sing "I gotta be me" or "I did it my way." In the Mediterranean world, everyone needs to know, "Who do others say that I am?" (Mark 8:27). It is critically important to meet and measure up to the expectations of the group and never to frustrate or surpass those expectations. The stubborn and rebellious son will be killed (Deut 21:18-21).

A Western person who hears these biblical exhortations to take up one's cross and deny one's self generally initiates a personal and individual plan of asceticism and penitential behaviors. The Mediterranean person who hears these same exhortations, like Jesus' immediate disciples and his medieval disciple Francis of Assisi, will sever ties with blood relatives but seek to join another group. Mediterranean people simply cannot exist without a group of one kind or another.

By leaving his family and village and travelling from place to place (Mark 1:38), Jesus effectively rejected the honor ascribed to him by birth (Mark 6:1-6). His teaching and healing activities and other behavior deviated from what his culture might expect from someone of his origins.

Summoning twelve followers (Mark 3:13-19), Jesus created a new fictive family group around himself. Then Jesus redefined the family by asserting, "Whoever does the will of God is my brother, and sister, and mother" (Mark 3:31-35). The questions Jesus poses to his followers in today's gospel (vv. 27-30) are an effort to learn his new honor status both among the general public and among his new kin. The answer (Messiah) reconfirms his status and authority to proclaim the reign of God.

Against this background, Jesus' exhortation to sever ties with other groups and become loyally attached to him and his group is powerfully impressive. Americans who belong to groups only so long as they are personally fulfilling will have to think twice.

Twenty-Fifth Sunday
in Ordinary Time
Mark 9:30-37

The scene of Jesus embracing a child, surrounded by his disciples who have just been squabbling over the appropriate pecking order of honor within their group, has been represented in art many times. Art, as we know, often reflects the culture of the artist much more than the cultural setting of the subject. At other times, art idealizes reality.

CHILDREN

In antiquity, childhood was a time of terror. Infant mortality rates sometimes reached 30 percent of live births. Sixty percent were dead by the age of sixteen. These figures reflect not only the ravages of unconquered diseases but also the outcomes of poor hygiene.

Moreover, while Western cultures tend to place children first and risk everything to save the child above all, ancient Middle Eastern cultures would place the child last. The medieval Mediterranean theologian Thomas Aquinas taught that in a raging fire a husband was obliged to save his father first, then his mother, next his wife, and last of all his young child. When a famine came upon the land, children would be fed last, after the adults. Such priorities are still common in many non-Western cultures.

Within the family and the community, the child had next to no status. A minor child was considered equal to a slave. Only after reaching maturity did a child become a free person with rights to inherit the family estate. When Jesus compares his adult compatriots to children who do not know how to respond to cultural cues (Matt 11:16-19), he effectively insults them.

Proverbs and Sirach exhort fathers to punish sons physically because they are considered basically evil and need strong correction if the father does not want to suffer neglect and abuse later in life (Prov 13:24; 19:18; 22:15; 23:13-14; 29:15, 17, 19; Sir 30:1-13).

This does not mean that children were not loved or appreciated. Mediterranean discipline fuses love with violence as parents explain: "We only do this because we love them." Even God disciplines "him whom he loves, and chastises every son whom he receives" (Prov 3:11-12).

Children are loved because they provide "social security" for parents. Obviously if they survive to adulthood, they also assure family continuity. Children are so greatly desired in the family that a wife will never be fully accepted into the patriarchal family setting until she bears a child, preferably a son. The emotional bond between that son and his mother is the strongest of all ties in the typical Mediterranean family.

Against this background, Jesus' statements in today's gospel take on fresh meaning. In verses 30-32, Jesus for the second time speaks to his disciples of impending betrayal, death, and return to life. Mark notes that they did not understand, and very likely they could not understand the combination of all these elements in a single statement.

There is no difficulty understanding betrayal leading to death. In the Mediterranean world, one would try to thwart such a plan but if that were impossible, the honorable person would strive to die in manly fashion. Rising to new life muddies the picture. Yet the disciples were afraid to ask Jesus for enlightenment.

HONOR IN A FACTION

Since Jesus' announcement has to do with his honor, it is no surprise that the disciples engage in a squabble over their honor in his group. The surprise again is Jesus' response to their squabble. Jesus' question is superfluous. No one whispers in this culture, and squabbles over honor would be quite vociferous. To pose the question bluntly as Jesus does is his first move in shaming the disciples. But Jesus doesn't stop there.

By asking the disciples to extend hospitality ("to welcome") a child, a creature of low status in their culture, Jesus further shames these grown men. Hospitality is extended to complete strangers to guarantee safe transit in unfamiliar and hostile territory. To extend hospitality to children ("to welcome them") would be a laugh to everyone else in the culture. Further, though guests are not expected to reciprocate hospitality, they are expected to broadcast the kindness of the host far and wide, thus extending his honorable reputation. Unpredictable children couldn't be counted upon to do that, so why bother?

Jesus teaches that life is full of surprises. True honor can be found in the most unlikely places.

Twenty-Sixth Sunday in Ordinary Time
Mark 9:38-43, 45, 47-48

Experts agree that Mediterranean culture is group centered. A pivotal virtue in such societies is loyalty to the group and its leader. The Greek and Hebrew word ordinarily translated as "faith" should more appropriately be translated "loyalty." This concept is evident in today's reading even though the word "faith" or "loyalty" is not explicitly used.

GROUP LOYALTY

Groups gather around a leader, and group members pledge and display their loyalty to that leader. The disciples of Jesus want to safeguard the distinct identity and prerogatives of their group. Thus, they do not deny that a nonmember of their group can cast out demons, but if he uses Jesus' name he should join the group and pledge loyalty to its leader. If not, he ought to stop using Jesus' name. That is the normative perspective in a group-centered society.

Jesus broadens the notion of loyalty. In his judgment, there is no reason why people not of his group cannot be loyal to him and act in his name. "Whoever is not against us is for us" (v. 40). (The very use of "us" again reflects the group focus.)

IMPORTANCE OF LOYALTY

In recent years, "kiss and tell" books have become an American political fashion. Friends of a president who served by appointment in his administration feel perfectly free to tell all sorts of stories when their appointment is completed. In the American cultural value system, loyalty is provisional and pragmatic.

The remaining verses of today's gospel passage display a radically different idea of loyalty in the Mediterranean world. The people whose loyalty is of concern to Jesus are the "little ones" who believe in (are loyal to) him (v. 42). Thus, the "little ones" are not children but rather adult followers of Jesus whom he sometimes calls children (Mark 10:24; cf. Matt 11:25).

Jesus' concern about those who cause his "little ones" to "sin" is a concern about those who rupture the faithfulness or loyalty of those little ones to him. Jesus considers unshaken loyalty to him so important that anyone who might disrupt it deserves capital punishment (being drowned with a stone tied around one's neck).

The comments of Jesus about sources of disruption to personal loyalty reflect first-century Mediterranean psychology, which is not at all introspective but rather based on values attributed to external dimensions of human life.

From the beginning to the end of the Bible, it is clear that the Hebrews viewed human beings as consisting of three interlocking zones symbolized by parts of the body. Hands and feet symbolize purposeful activity. If one's activity (hand or foot) causes one to stumble during tests of loyalty, one must put an end to such behavior.

Eyes are invariably paired with the heart in the Bible to symbolize the zone of emotion-fused thought, reflective consideration of proper courses of action. If the eye, the organ that feeds information to the heart, is unreliable in tests of loyalty, one must take serious action to halt the damage.

Interpreters incline toward giving these verses figurative rather than literal meaning. Surely Jesus did not intend to gather a band of lame and blind followers around himself. While this view has merit, one should not forget that even today in the Middle East physical punishment of this sort is still meted out to convicted criminals.

Jesus' point is that no matter how painful, any effort to insure loyalty to him in this life is far less painful than the punishment for disloyalty to be administered in the world to come.

The seriousness of Jesus' exhortation becomes painfully apparent in the accounts of his crucifixion and death. Judean authorities who conspired to have Jesus put to death stand by the cross and mock him, saying: "He rescued others, but he cannot rescue himself. *If* he comes down from the cross now, we will place our loyalty and faithfulness in him" (see Mark 15:32; Matt 27:42).

Mediterranean loyalty means "faithfulness no matter what." It challenges the conditional loyalty proposed by the authorities to Jesus on the cross and the American idea of pragmatic loyalty. What does loyalty mean to you?

Twenty-Seventh Sunday in Ordinary Time
Mark 10:2-16

THE HONOR OF JESUS

Nearly every question in the Mediterranean world is a challenge. This is why Jesus usually responds with a counterchallenge, most often an insult. The insult here is "you," indicating that Jesus distances himself from his hostile questioners ("Is it lawful?") and their interpretation of the Law.

MARRIAGE AND DIVORCE IN JESUS' WORLD

In the ancient Mediterranean world, marriages were between families. Each family selected a partner, union with whom was intended to bind the families together, forming a stronger unit. Just as children cannot choose their parents, so too children in this culture could not choose their marriage partners. God chose one's parents, and through one's parents God chose one's marriage partner. Hence Jesus' cultural truism about marriage: "What God has joined together, let no one separate" (v. 9).

Even such a brief statement of the nature of Mediterranean marriages makes it evident why divorce would be unacceptable. Divorce is not just the separation of two partners but rather the separation of two families. In a society driven by the values of honor and shame, the family of the bride will be shamed. The bride's male relatives in particular will have to bear the shame as well as the responsibility to remedy it. Feuding will result and undoubtedly escalate to bloodshed.

This must be avoided at all cost, hence the cultural rule is no divorce.

COMPLICATING FACTORS

In his private explanation to the disciples, Jesus adds one complication to the discussion: remarriage. The discussion is not simply about divorce, which though bad enough was permitted by the Law of Moses (see v. 4). The problem hinges on divorce and remarriage (vv. 10-11).

Moreover, Mark's community apparently is familiar with a situation in which the woman or woman's family can initiate the divorce. This affront to the husband's family is so shameful that it must necessarily result in feuding.

Within this social system, remarriage necessarily entails adultery. But the situation is drastically different from that supposed in contemporary Western notions of divorce and adultery. In the Middle Eastern world, adultery is the strategy by which one male shames another male, namely the husband of the wife who is a partner in the adultery.

A wife cannot commit adultery. Culturally it is impossible for her to shame a man's wife. If a husband has relations with any female (even a prostitute) other than his wife, he does not and cannot shame his honorable wife. Only males can be shamed.

What then does it mean when Mark's Jesus says, "Whoever divorces his wife and marries another commits adultery *against her?*" From the Mediterranean cultural perspective, the shame must reflect upon a male, and the males would be the wife's father, brothers, or other significant men in her family. Because of the inevitable bloodshed, such a situation must be avoided at all costs.

The behaviors prohibited in the Ten Commandments are precisely affronts of males against other males which require vengeance. Hence the basic purpose of the commandments in ancient Israelite society was to head off feuding which led to bloodshed. The idea was to maintain internal societal harmony and stability.

CHILDREN

Children were the walking newspapers of that time. They were trained by their families and permitted by other families to roam freely in and out of homes to spy on what other families were doing. Attempts to keep children away from Jesus would stir suspicion that he was up to no good and intent on harming others. Jesus insists he has nothing to hide. Let the children snoop.

Second, and perhaps more important here, the mothers want Jesus to touch their children. In the ancient Mediterranean world, almost 30 percent of live births were dead by the age of six. Sixty percent were gone by the age of sixteen. Jesus' touch would ward off the "evil eye," that is, malicious envy by others that could inflict sickness and death.

How might this gospel episode help Americans to find relief from the pressures of their culture such as Jesus remedied in his?

Twenty-Eighth Sunday in Ordinary Time
Mark 10:17-30

COMPLIMENT

The questioner in this instance is not hostile, but his greeting, "Good Master," signals aggression. Compliments in this culture imply that the complimented person has tried to rise above others, to their detriment. In this society, when one person gets ahead everyone else is considered to have fallen behind.

Further, paying a compliment so publicly and without precaution borders on revealing "the evil eye." One can frequently suspect that the questioner envies the named qualities in the other person (goodness), and secretly wishes they would be destroyed.

Jesus sizes up the scene perfectly and responds with appropriate and expected cultural "humility." He denies the compliment and successfully defuses any threat to social order that listeners might perceive in the compliment.

CHALLENGE

Mark alone mentions that Jesus "loved him" (v. 21; cf. Matt 19:16-30 and Luke 18:18-30). "Love" in Mediterranean culture is appropriately translated as "attachment" in an active and practical way. The youth's claim that he lived a well-rounded moral life "since my youth" stirs Jesus' affection toward the lad to the degree that he would like to have the young man join him and his disciples.

148

Jesus' familiar advice, however, needs to be distanced from the economic interpretation Westerners usually attribute to it. "Go sell what you have" means to part with the most precious of all possessions in the Mediterranean world: family, home, and land. It is not primarily cashing in one's stock portfolio, emptying the bank account, and disposing of other similar Western treasures.

In order to follow Jesus, one must break blood ties with one's family, as the disciples have already done. This is spelled out quite explicitly in Jesus' reflection upon Peter's statement that the disciples "have left everything." Jesus says, "There is no one who has left house or brothers or sisters or mother or father or children or lands for my sake and the gospel" who will not be compensated (v. 29).

In a society where family and kinship ties are essential conditions for life itself, Jesus' challenge amounts to social suicide. His exhortation is morally impossible to fulfill without some compensating factors.

Jesus states these immediately. The young man will have "treasure in heaven," that is, God will replace the sources of sustenance that this person willingly sacrifices. And "come follow me" promises him fellowship in a new community, a fictive family to replace his family of flesh and blood. This is what Jesus has been creating throughout this gospel.

The young man certainly perceived that Jesus desired him to join the group and clearly understood the sacrifice Jesus demanded (but would replace). With regret and sorrow, he rejects both of Jesus' offers and departs, "for he had great possessions."

WEALTH AND GREED

The conclusion of this episode instructs us about the ancient Mediterranean understanding of the word "rich." Possessions did not constitute a problem for this man. It was his unwillingness to share that caused the problem, to give to those who had less than he ("the poor"). For this reason, wherever the word "rich" appears in the Bible it is more appropriately rendered "greedy." This man was not simply rich but also "greedy" (cf. Luke 12:13-21).

The disciples are shocked to hear that the greedy rich have no advantage when it comes to dealing with God. "Who then can be saved?" In Mediterranean culture, the greedy rich want for nothing because they surround themselves with clients who supply their needs, including the need for honorable reputation. Clients spread the word about their benefactor and their good fortune. Jesus says all this counts for nothing with God.

Those like Jesus' followers who have severed ties with blood relationships and freely embraced a reversal of status in a society which thrives on status will receive a double reward: a hundredfold return "with persecutions" in this life, and eternal life in the age to come.

Status reversal sounds great to those whose status is raised but prompts a violent response from those who are toppled from their honorable position. How does the promise of Jesus in this episode resonate with American concern for immediate gratification and a here-and-now pay-off?

Twenty-Ninth Sunday in Ordinary Time
Mark 10:35-45

ACQUIRING HONOR

The group that Jesus gathered around himself is technically called a faction. Members of such a group each have a direct, important, and relatively strong relationship with the leader but very little knowledge of or relationship with each other.

In today's story, James and John, two blood relatives, do something very normal and customary in this culture within factions. They jockey for a higher position of honor in the group and care nothing about the others. When Jesus receives his full measure of honor, these two brothers want a share in it by gaining the most prestigious positions next to him. In this culture, everything is always about honor.

Each group member already possesses a degree of honor that derives from birth. Nothing can be added to or subtracted from that honor. Thus, Jesus from Nazareth is an artisan's son. Simon and Andrew are sons of Jonah, as James and John are sons of Zebedee.

But honor can also be achieved, most often through honor contests known as "challenge and riposte." One person asks another questions in hopes of shaming him and thereby increasing his own honor. The request of James and John is still another way of achieving honor: personal effort. Here, the effort is little more than the request for a favor.

Since Jesus is the acknowledged leader of this group, he can do a favor for individual members and grant them privileges that would make them stand out in relationship to others. Of course, the others are incensed to learn of this move and express indignation (v. 41).

ASSIGNING HONOR

Instead of granting the favor, Jesus asks if the brothers "can drink the cup" that he drinks which constitutes his claim to achieved honor. Like all metaphors, this one, too, developed from a real-life custom. In Mediterranean culture, the head of the family fills the cups of all at table. Each one is expected to accept and drink what the head of the family has given. Since all theology is based on analogy, and the behavior of God is assumed to be like the behavior of human beings in a given culture, the cup came to represent the lot in life which God has assigned for each person (see Pss 11:6; 16:5; 23:5; etc.).

If Jesus accepts his assigned lot, he will attain the honor determined by God (Mark 14:36). The brothers impetuously affirm that they can indeed accept and fulfill the same lot assigned to Jesus.

At this point, Jesus reminds them that he is a broker in the kingdom and not its patron. Jesus can put others in touch with God the patron, but it is God alone who determines each person's lot and deserved honor.

A NEW WAY

Continuing his reflection on true honor, Jesus invites the entire faction to reflect upon life as they know it. The Mediterranean "outsiders" (non-Judean rulers and great men) know how to determine personal status and how to behave accordingly. Rulers "lord it" over their subjects because this is how one exercises authority.

Jesus proposes a different way for renewed Israel, the way of status reversal. The great ones in this community should behave like servants at ceremonial meals, that is, like deacons. Those who hold positions of primacy should consider their status as equal to that of slaves.

The reason for this new rule in determining true honor in the Jesus movement lies in the behavior of the "son of Man" who served (played the role of deacon) and "gave his life as a ransom" so that others could be set free (see also 1 Tim 2:6).

What would prompt an invading power or an oppressor to accept one hostage and let others go free? Only the fact that the hostage was of higher status. An invading power would gladly accept a prince or king as hostage and let the peasant go free. There is more prestige to holding, and perhaps executing, royalty than slaughtering large numbers of peasants. In the game of chess, capturing the king ends the game even if all other pieces are still on the board.

If someone of Jesus' high status sacrificed himself for the benefit of others not so highly honored, how would such logic translate itself into American politics or the American Church?

Thirtieth Sunday in Ordinary Time
Mark 10:46-52

BLINDNESS IN ANTIQUITY

Blindness was very common in the ancient Middle East. Most cases were due to trachoma, a contagious infection of the inner mucous lining of the eyelids (the conjunctiva) and of the cornea. The disease was transmitted by flies and by poor hygiene. A simple practice like washing one's hands would have helped, but scarcity of water prompted many peasants to omit even required ritual ablutions (possibly the occasion for the Pharisees' objection in Mark 7:1-5).

The real bane of blindness in ancient Israel seems to be the awareness that God who bestows this gift also withholds it or takes it away (Exod 4:11). In some though not all instances, loss of sight was associated with displeasing God, that is, sin (Gen 19:11; Deut 28:28; 2 Kgs 6:18; Acts 13:11). Tobit and the man born blind in John 9 illustrate exceptions to this belief.

Yet despite the pain deriving from knowing that for some mysterious reason God has deprived one of sight, a blind person did not feel cursed. In Genesis (1:3-5), God existed in darkness before creating light. Darkness therefore symbolizes the presence of God. To live in darkness, that is being unable to see, is to live in the presence of God. Such intimacy with God compensates the blind person who can interact with but not see other human beings who are created in the image and likeness of God (Gen 1:26).

154

THE BLIND BEGGAR

Even though blind, the beggar in Mark's Gospel is very shrewd. He has heard of Jesus' reputation as a folk healer. How can he "force" Jesus to heal him?

He bases his request to Jesus on "mercy" (vv. 47-48). "Son of David, have mercy on me!" In the Mediterranean value system, mercy describes a person's willingness to pay personal debts. By repeating this statement over and over, the beggar insists that Jesus owes the healing to him. By shouting it out ever more loudly, the clever beggar makes the entire crowd aware of Jesus' debt to him.

On what basis does Jesus owe this apparent stranger anything? By addressing him as "son of David," the beggar publicly identifies Jesus as Messiah (as "son of David" is interpreted in Mark's Gospel). Even if Jesus or the crowd were to disagree about messianic imputation, the title "son of David" situates Jesus in the lineage which includes Solomon, a near omniscient and omnicompetent ruler. It would be very difficult indeed for Jesus to accept either honorific accolade without rewarding the person who announced them.

The beggar regains his sight and immediately follows Jesus. Such a response is not unusual but rather quite in line with the Mediterranean institution of patronage. Jesus, of course, is the broker and not the patron. He is the one who has ready access to God, the patron, and who can connect clients like the blind beggar with God the patron. The healed beggar joins Jesus' entourage because he is indebted to Jesus and will sing his—and the patron's—praises far and wide. A favor received is a favor owed, even if the return favor is not expected.

By setting this story in his Gospel right after Jesus contrasts the behavior of non-Judean rulers with those who hold authority in the Jesus movement, Mark invites the reader further to reflect on the difference. Jesus the folk healer is located by his would-be client in the royal lineage of David. But instead of "lording it over" his beneficiary, Jesus adopts the role of servant, accedes to the blind man's request, intercedes—like a servant—with the God of Israel, and obtains restoration of the man's sight. The beggar in turn feels bound to point to Jesus as his successful broker with the patron-God of Israel who does not turn a deaf ear to the requests of a humble subject.

Americans who tire of wrestling with the Mediterranean core value of honor Sunday by Sunday in the Gospels have a golden opportunity in today's gospel to compare its effectiveness in the ancient healing system with the workings of the contemporary health care system.

Thirty-First Sunday in Ordinary Time
Mark 12:28-34

LOVE, HATE, AND GROUP ATTACHMENT

The scribe who asks Jesus "which commandment is first of all?" is not hostile. His question is not a test or a trap but rather the solicitation of an opinion. Whatever Jesus answers can be the topic for further discussion.

This is also one of the rare times when Jesus answers a question directly and quickly: "Love the Lord God above all, and love your neighbor as yourself." Jesus weaves together two elements of his tradition: Deuteronomy 6:5 and Leviticus 19:18. Familiar as this answer is to modern believers, the word "love" and its correlative "hate" carry different meanings in the Mediterranean world than they do in the modern Western world.

For modern, introspective, individualistic Western believers, these words relate to internal, psychological states. They invariably entail feeling, emotion, affection.

In the ancient, non-introspective, group-centered Mediterranean world, these words involved primarily an external, concrete expression. Affection, emotion, feeling may or may not have been involved. The concrete, external expression of love is attachment to one's group or attachment to a person in the group. It is the kinship group, the village group, or the faction group that one joined at some point in life that mattered above all.

To love God above all means to become attached exclusively to Yahweh-God to the exclusion of any and all other deities. It would also entail attaching oneself to the group that clusters itself distinctly around this God.

To love one's neighbor as oneself means to become exclusively attached to the people in one's own neighborhood or village as if they were family. The full context of Leviticus 19:18 which Mark's Jesus quotes makes it quite clear that "neighbor" means "fellow ethnic." "You shall not take vengeance or bear any grudge against the sons of your own people, but you shall love your neighbor as yourself: I am the Lord."

This same idea characterizes "hate," the correlative of love. Luke's Jesus says, "If anyone comes to me and does not hate his own father and mother and wife and children and brothers and sisters, yes and even his own life, he cannot be my disciple" (14:26). Jesus is not commanding his followers to cultivate a negative emotion toward their intimate kinfolk but rather to detach themselves from the kinship group "for the sake of Jesus and the gospel" and join the Jesus movement.

The depth of detachment required of a follower of Jesus is expressed in the varying reports of Peter's dialogue with Jesus. In Matthew (19:27) and Mark (10:28) Peter says, "We have left everything to follow you." Luke specifies "everything" when Peter says, "Lo, we have left our homes and followed you" (18:28). Because one's very life depends upon loyalty and attachment to the family, to leave home and kin is to leave everything meaningful in life, to risk death itself (see Luke 15:17).

The scribe who perfectly understands the cultural meanings just sketched wholeheartedly agrees and adds, "this is 'much more' than all whole burnt offerings and sacrifices" (v. 33). Jesus approves his wise answer and grants him a public mark of honor that surely impressed the audience: "you are very close to enjoying God's favor."

The kind of group attachment that characterized the cultural world of Jesus is highly desired but difficult to attain in Western culture. As precious a cultural value as it is, Western individualism proves to be the biggest obstacle to community. Westerners tend to be very pragmatic with regard to group attachment. They join a group and remain members only as long as the group meets their personal needs. When it fails to do so, they drop out and join another group on similar terms.

In recent years, North Americans have been impressed with the small-group movement in Central and South America and attempted to replicate this reality in the United States. A Princeton University study of this phenomenon recently concluded that instead of fostering community the small-group movement in the United States increased individualism.

No one had noticed that small groups in Latin cultures play a moderating role in the face of the potentially suffocating results of group attachment on a large scale. It is risky to import institutions and values across cultures without properly understanding them.

Thirty-Second Sunday in Ordinary Time
Mark 12:38-44

SCRIBES

In a public place and likely within earshot of his targets, Jesus hurls a scathing insult at the scribes by urging the crowd to be wary of them. The scribes of Jesus' day were experts in the Law of Moses, scholars to whom people turned for proper understanding of God's will as revealed in Scripture. They contributed to the development of rabbinism in the third century of the common era, the forerunner of modern-day Judaism.

Jesus publicly criticizes their behavior as a ceaseless grasping for honor. The Talmud notes that when two people meet in the marketplace, the one inferior in knowledge of the Law should greet the other first. Since no one knew the Law as well as the scribes, they sought out and basked in this recognition.

In the synagogue the scribes claimed the best seats which were those on a platform facing the people. People seated on these chairs rested their backs against the same wall that held the ark which contained the Torah scrolls.

At banquets, the best seats were reserved for people of importance like experts in the Law.

Jesus concludes his attack by accusing the scribes of "devouring widows' houses." No sooner has Jesus spoken than a widow comes along and places two of the smallest coins in first-century Palestine into the coffers, thus fulfilling her religious duty.

WIDOWS

Jesus' comment on the widow's donation is not a word of praise but rather a word of lament: "Truly I say to you this poor widow has put in more than all those who are contributing to the treasury. For they all contributed out of their abundance; but she out of her poverty has put in everything she had, her whole living" (Mark 12:43-44).

The word for "widow" in Hebrew carries the meaning of one who is silent, who is unable to speak. Recall that all of Mediterranean culture is divided along gender lines. Men belong in the public sphere; women remain secluded with the children deep within the home. Men play the public role, and women do not speak on their own behalf.

A widow is already bereft of her husband, the male in whom she was embedded. If her eldest son was not yet married, she was even more disadvantaged. And if she had no sons at all, she might have to return to her family of origin (see Lev 22:13; Ruth 1:8) if that were still possible. As the Pastoral Epistles indicate, widows constituted a major concern in the early Christian community. Younger ones posed a special danger, and the author of those Epistles urged them to remarry (1 Tim 5:3-16, esp. v. 14).

Because widows were not included in Hebrew inheritance laws, their constant concern was simply living from day to day. Any resources this widow had were meager at best. In the Mediterranean world, the cultural obligation upon everybody is to maintain one's status and do nothing to jeopardize or lessen it. If, as Jesus observes, this woman has given to the Temple "all she had to live on," the woman has acted very shamefully. She has deliberately worsened her status.

Earlier in this Gospel Jesus said it is wrong to donate to the Temple while depriving one's parents of support (Mark 7:10-13 on the "qorban"). It would be doubly wrong for a needy person to donate to the Temple and plunge only deeper into poverty.

Further, how could Jesus in good conscience praise this woman for donating "everything she had" to the Temple which in the very next verses Jesus predicts will be utterly destroyed? "Not one stone will be left here upon another; all will be thrown down" (13:2). Such perversity ill becomes a teacher who earned a reputation for compassion.

Jesus does not praise but rather laments this woman's behavior. She has been taught "sacrificial giving" by her religious leaders, and that is the pity. These authorities promised to redistribute Temple collections to the needy. In actuality, they spent the funds on conspicuous consumption instead: long robes and banquets. This is how they "devoured the estates of widows" (Mark 12:40).

Occasional scandals in American churches suggest that little has changed over the centuries. Responsible stewardship is everyone's obligation.

Thirty-Third Sunday in Ordinary Time
Mark 13:24-32

RELIGION OR POLITICS?

To place today's gospel reading in focus, it is important to remember that in ancient Israel there were only two formal (i.e., free-standing) social institutions: kinship (family and family-like groups) and politics. The distinct social institutions recognized by modern Western culture as economics, education, and religion were embedded in those first two.

Thus, education took place within the family for the purpose of enculturating youngsters into proper ways of living and behaving as family members. Education also took place in the royal court to train individuals for roles in the palace: courtier, diplomat, etc.

Religion, too, was embedded in family and in politics. Family religion was rather private and focused on concern for ancestors and household gods (see Gen 31:34-35). Political religion was quite public and took place in the Temple through regular services, occasional pilgrimage feasts, and the like. That politics and religion were "identical" in ancient Israel is evident in the fact that the Hebrew language uses just one word for "palace" and "Temple."

By predicting the imminent destruction of the Temple (Mark 13:1-2), Jesus announces the end of political Israel and the political institution in which it was embedded. Today's verses which are carved from the totality of chapter 13 focus on God's role in this event. The cosmic events (darkening of the sun and moon, stars falling from heaven, and shaking of the powers in the heavens) are entirely and exclusively under God's control. No one else can manipulate these elements of creation (vv. 24-25).

The next verses (26-27) echo descriptions of an official visit of an emperor, technically called a *parousia* in Greek. Roads are prepared for the entourage: potholes are filled in and chariot ruts are leveled (Isa 40:3-4, "every mountain and hill will be made low, and rough places a plain").

Messengers announce the coming of the emperor (Isa 52:7, "how beautiful upon the mountains are the feet of him who brings good tidings") and gather the people to greet him (v. 27). Great displays of power and honor are a very important part of the announcement.

WHEN IS THE END?

Mark's Jesus is absolutely convinced that everything he has announced will occur during the lifetime of his audience. We know Jesus died around 30 C.E., and the Temple was destroyed in 70 C.E. That Jesus survived birth and lived approximately to the age of thirty places him in a very select 10 percent of the population of his time and place. A large portion of Jesus' audience would have been considerably younger than he, severely disease-ridden, and facing ten or fewer years of life-expectancy. In the light of this data from paleopathology (the study of ancient disease), it would seem Jesus expected the political end of Israel much sooner than it actually occurred.

He is so positive that he gives his word of honor: "Truly, I tell you" and "Heaven and earth will pass away but my words will not pass away" (vv. 30-31). Secrecy, lying, and deception are so integral a part of safeguarding Mediterranean honor that people are at a loss to know when someone is telling the truth. To guarantee the truth of what one says, a person swears an oath: "By my life," "As I live," "Truly, Truly I say to you," and the like.

Another way to guarantee the truth of one's statement is to say, "even if the impossible should happen, what I tell you is impossible not to happen. Heaven and earth are God's good creation and will last forever. Even if you can imagine the impossible (that they will disappear), my impossible sounding statement is definitely going to occur."

Westerners love to plan for the future. They invented future planning, believing they can estimate and cause events to take place within the next five to twenty-five years. Like the disciples, they too would like to know and try to calculate when "the end" will happen. As the year 2000 approaches, many Christians are attempting to make a similar guess-timate.

Everyone needs to re-read Jesus' final words: "No one knows, neither the angels in heaven, nor the Son, but only the Father" (Mark 13:32). And he's not telling!

Thirty-Fourth Sunday
in Ordinary Time
(Christ the King)
John 18:33-37

KINGSHIP AND POLITICS

John 18:28–19:16 is the centerpiece of John's passion narrative. It can be structured into seven scenes by attending to the shifts from outside (e.g., 18:28-32) to inside (e.g., 33-38a). In the central scene (19:1-3), the soldiers mock Jesus and call him derisively "King of the Judeans." In John's Gospel, people who speak in irony frequently speak the truth. Jesus is indeed king! But what does this mean? John's Jesus will explain.

In today's verses, one cultural element that stands out is Jesus' sarcastic responses to the procurator Pilate. When asked point-blank whether he is "King of the Judeans" Jesus asks Pilate whether he is personally interested or is simply repeating gossip. When Pilate attempts to conclude from Jesus' explanation that he is indeed a king, Jesus again sidesteps by responding: "That's what *you* say!"

Placing this dialogue in a cultural light shows Pilate to be somewhat restrained. Being of higher status and different ethnic background than Jesus, Pilate did not have to put up with wisecracks. Still, whether he liked this dialogue or not, Pilate had to determine whether Jesus posed any real threat to Rome. Weak-spined Roman sycophant that he was, Pilate seems nevertheless to have been genuinely curious about Jesus.

Jesus separates his rightful status from the political realm into which it has been cast by his accusers. "My kingship is not of this world" (v. 36). If Jesus had political aspirations, his subjects would have fought against his arrest. This is not the arena in which he consciously chooses to defend himself.

KINGSHIP AND TRUTH

Jesus prefers instead to be known as one who "bears witness to the truth." In John's Gospel, Jesus doesn't preach the kingdom of God or of heaven as in the Synoptics. John rather presents Jesus as one who uniquely reveals and speaks the truth about God. Like the prophets of old, John's Jesus speaks the will of God for the here-and-now.

Jesus' followers are not subjects in a kingdom but persons who hear the truth and respond to it. It is in this and not in a political sense that Jesus can be understood as king and possessing a kingdom. Jesus concludes his comment to Pilate with a veiled challenge: "Everyone who is of the truth hears my voice." The implicit challenge is clear to Pilate: "Will you listen to me and accept the truth, God's plan for salvation?" Pilate chooses to evade the challenge: "Truth, eh? What is that?"

This gospel makes a very appropriate conclusion to the Sundays of this cycle and their Scripture readings. Sunday after Sunday, believers have heard Jesus' witness to the truth in the gospels and learned the power of its cultural impact in these reflections and in the homily. Jesus' challenge to Pilate challenges modern believers as well: "Every one who is of the truth hears my voice." Have you heard and responded to the voice of Jesus?

KING BEFORE TIME

Celebrating this particular Sunday as the feast of Christ the King offers yet another challenge to believers, particularly those who live in a democracy. Since its founding as a republic, the United States vigorously rejected any effort to impose a king's rule over it. They would not accept King George of England, nor would they crown George Washington as king either.

Jesus denied kingship in the political sense, too. The kingship celebrated today is a theological construct contributed to the Church in part by Franciscan theology.

The Franciscans who helped develop this observance called it "the feast of the absolute predestination of Christ." Taking their cue from texts like Colossians 1:15, they reasoned that Christ was the firstborn of all creation. God who exists outside of time knows the existence of all creation at once. To create the first flesh-and-blood human in the divine image and likeness, God needed a flesh-and-blood model. Jesus incarnate was that model. This is how the Franciscans understood the kingship of Christ.

Clearly, American believers cannot blindly imitate their Mediterranean ancestors in the faith. Only after grasping the cultural dimensions of their ancestors' beliefs can Americans begin to translate and incarnate those insights into their own distinctive culture, Sunday by Sunday.

Recommended Readings

Dunning, James B. *Echoing God's Word*. Arlington, Va.: The North American Forum on the Catechumenate, 1992.

Elliott, John H. *What Is Social-Scientific Criticism?* Minneapolis: Fortress, 1993.

Esler, Philip F., ed. *Modelling Early Christianity: Social Scientific Studies of the New Testament in Its Context*. London and New York: Routledge, 1995.

Hanson, K. C. *Pentecost 3*. Proclamation 4: Aids for Interpreting the Lesson of the Church Year, Series B. Minneapolis: Fortress, 1991. (Twentieth to the Last Sunday after Pentecost, cycle B, in social scientific perspective.)

Malina, Bruce J., and Richard L. Rohrbaugh. *Social-Science Commentary on the Synoptic Gospels*. Minneapolis: Fortress, 1992.

Malina, Bruce J. *Windows on the World of Jesus: Time Travel to Ancient Judea*. Louisville: Westminster/John Knox Press, 1993.

Malina, Diane Jacobs. *Beyond Patriarchy: The Images of Family in Jesus*. New York/Mahwah: Paulist Press, 1993.

Neyrey, Jerome H., S.J. *The Resurrection Stories*. Zacchaeus Studies: New Testament. Collegeville, Minn: The Liturgical Press, A Michael Glazier Book, 1988.

Pilch, Jean Peters. "Planning–Mark." *Celebration: An Ecumenical Worship Resource* 23 (1994) passim.

Pilch, John J., and Bruce J. Malina, eds. *Biblical Social Values and the Meaning: A Handbook*. Peabody, Mass.: Hendrickson, 1993.

Pilch, John J. "Jews and Christians: Anachronisms in Biblical Translations." *Professional Approaches for Christian Educators [PACE].* April 1996.

_____. "Death with Honor: The Mediterranean Style Death of Jesus in Mark." *Biblical Theology Bulletin* 25 (1995) 65–70.

_____. "Illuminating the World of Jesus through Cultural Anthropology." *The Living Light* 31 (1994) 20–31.

_____. *The Triduum: Breaking Open the Scriptures of Holy Week.* Columbus: Initiatives Publications, 1993.